I Called Him Grand Dad

I Called Him Grand Dad

Thomas T. Fields, Jr.

Library of Congress Control Number:		2009904559
ISBN:	Hardcover	978-1-4415-3540-5
	Softcover	978-1-4415-3539-9

This book was printed in the United States of America.

To order additional copies of this book, contact:
Xlibris Corporation
1-888-795-4274
www.Xlibris.com
Orders@Xlibris.com
59236

CONTENTS

ACKNOWLEDGEMENT

This book is dedicated to my mother, Ruth Katherine, who taught me to seek knowledge and who patiently took the time and effort to save the papers of Harvey Fields. Thanks to my co-workers Don, Cheryl, Jon, Crissie and Karen who have supported me so much. Special thanks to my principal, Mr. Clinton, Coach Carpenter and Scout Master Holder. A hug for my wife Bonnie, and kids Sarah, Tommy and Chris for tolerating me and of course Harvey and his son, my father, Thomas, Sr. Special acknowledgement to my friend for life, Steve and my Cousin Buddy.

INTRODUCTION

In 1961, I was ten years old. On a beautiful Easter day in North Louisiana, I ran next door to see if my grandfather felt better, and if he would join us for Easter lunch. Suddenly I froze at the door that led to his living room. A strange chill came over me, and I found I could not enter.

"You go in first," I told my father, who was trailing behind me. He did, and I peeked around the corner to see the little old man that I idolized sitting in his rocking chair, slurring his speech and trying to rise. Fifteen minutes later, he was being escorted to a car. He stopped and looked at my troubled face, managed a slight smile, and patted me on the head as if to say, "Don't worry, I will be all right."

This was the last time we communicated. Little did I realize at that time the life that this man had lived. He had dined with presidents and leaders of industry, was considered a legal genius, and spent a life in political and legal service to his state and country; but to me, he was simply Granddad.

He was born May 31, 1883, to the founder of the newspaper in Avoyelles Parish, Louisiana; his father had left Kentucky to move to Louisiana. At birth, he was given the name Harvey Goodwin Fields. Politics coupled with a keen sense of right and combined with a high need to achieve were in the genetics of Harvey. A cousin was elected governor of Kentucky in the 1920s, and he was a descendant of a settler that entered Kentucky with Daniel Boone. He had a burning desire to help the oppressed of his state and the nation and to raise the hopes of the laboring class during the most devastating economic time of the nation. Harvey was also a believer that the laws instituted by man superseded all else. He was a defender of the rights provided by these laws and spent his life upholding these principles. Fields's actions displayed the highest examples of honor and integrity, and his dedication to the tenets of his position ultimately led to the ire of state and federal officials.

In his later years of life, he would stay up all hours of the night, visiting one of the two small convenience stores in his hometown. He would sit for hours and tell stories well into the evening and provide insight on a previous life until it was time for the store to close. Occasionally, he would travel to South Louisiana, and Harvey was well known to many of the gas station attendants as he would break his trip for a gallon of gas and spend time visiting with the owners. This was a far cry from the numerous trips he had previously taken by train in the 1920s, '30s, and '40s to Washington to meet with dignitaries and consult on legal matters. Though age had caught up with Fields his love of people, coupled with his oratory abilities, never left him.

In 1900, he graduated from Marksville High School. Three years later, he graduated from Louisiana Polytechnic Institute (LPI). In 1905, he received his law degree from Tulane University Law School. That same year, he was appointed alderman for the town of Farmerville in rural North Louisiana. At the age of thirty, he was elected to the Louisiana senate. Fields served as Louisiana district attorney from 1921 to 1925. In 1925, he became chairman of the Louisiana Democratic State Central Committee. In 1928, he became a member of the Louisiana Public Service Commission and, the same year, led the delegation to the Democratic National Convention in Houston. In 1936, he relinquished the chairmanship of the commission to become the United States district attorney for the Western District of Louisiana. Fields continued to practice law until his death in 1961. In 1958, members of the Union Parish Bar Association presented him with the prestigious award for fifty years of practice in Union Parish.

During his career, he was a member of the Long, Fields and O'Neal Law Firm headed by Huey Long, with Earl Long also serving as a member.

When the Scopes Monkey Trial was held, he was there to see his two friends battle the legalities of evolution. When a standing governor broke the law, he prosecuted him. When Louisiana sent two delegations to the Democratic National Convention, he successfully pleaded the case of the delegation he headed to be seated. By the time I knew him, he had retired to become a small-town lawyer that still maintained the air of the old South and whose accomplishments were little known to the residents of Farmerville.

He had a unique sense of right. He embraced the doctrine of Huey Long when it came to providing support for the poor and giving every resident of Louisiana the opportunity to an education. He supported Franklin Roosevelt politically but fell out of favor with him on several New Deal policies. He was vocal on occasion when he felt that a policy was wrong or was not in the best interest of the common man. This disregard for political position when confronted with a moral issue ultimately led to his decline.

All this, and I only knew him as Granddad.

Harvey Fields died in 1961. Several files of his political papers were packed away following his death. For forty-five years, they remained untouched. In 2006, these documents were discovered. The content of these letters gives new insight into a time of tumultuous and fast-changing political landscapes in Louisiana and the United States. They bring to light an individual who fought for the rights of the oppressed, who believed in civil liberties, and who was a staunch supporter of the Constitution of the United States of America—a man whose values could not be compromised.

CHAPTER 1

THE EARLY YEARS
A DEGREE, A CONVENTION, AND A MONKEY

Harvey Fields was born on May 31, 1883, to the founder of the first newspaper in Avoyelles Parish, Louisiana. Fields's father had moved from Danville, Kentucky, to Marksville, Louisiana, with a dream of starting his own newspaper. The reason for this move is unclear; however, it is known that the family was prominent in Kentucky, and a relative had been with Daniel Boone when he entered Kentucky. The years following the Civil War were tough in many areas of the South, and families were forced to uproot and start new beginnings. Politics and public service were in the genetics of the family. Another cousin of Fields was elected governor of Kentucky, and other members of the family had entered politics and public service.

At the time of Fields's birth, the Civil War had been over for only eighteen years. The Reconstruction years in the South following the end of the war, coupled with retribution for the death of President Lincoln, had drastically curtailed the healing of the country. Residents of the states in the Deep South looked for leadership that would provide the basic needs for living. Leaders would emerge that were totally committed to providing a better society in which to live in. Others would emerge with the purpose of bettering their own personal position and wealth with very little regard for the working class. Many times, the two would clash.

Clubs, societies, and organizations were very important during this period of time. It was in these forums that the leadership would emerge that would carve the direction of the country. In Louisiana, the Democratic Party was unquestionably the dominant political party; however, the rules that dictated how Louisiana would live came from a series of political bosses across the state with the power base located in New Orleans. For the most part, the farmer in the fields and the laborer in the mills and the forester in the woods were not the predominate concern for these bosses.

Harvey Fields understood at an early age that the newspaper was a powerful tool. While he was growing up, there were only two methods for mass communications. These were the newspaper and public speaking. He had learned firsthand the art of journalism from his father. This early experience served him well throughout his career.

In 1900, he entered Louisiana State University (LSU) and attended classes for two years. He transferred to Louisiana Polytechnic Institute, now Louisiana Tech University, and received two degrees. One of these degrees was in journalism. While at LPI, Fields was displaying his desire to establish, arrange, and manage organizations. A letter from the president of LPI to Fields complimented him for his marked improvement in academics, but also denied the young Fields's request to form a secret club at the school.

Following his graduation from LPI, Fields entered Tulane University and graduated from the Tulane University Law School in 1905. Fields then entered law practice in Marksville and remained there for a short time. In 1905, Fields moved to Farmerville in rural North Louisiana, where he established his new practice.

In 1905, he also began his political career. That year, he was elected alderman in the town of Farmerville. He was also continually working within the Democratic Party. Fields was extremely competitive in all his endeavors. When Fields had a cause he felt was worth fighting for, he was relentless in driving it to success. If there was a case that he was involved with, he would do everything in his power to win. It didn't matter whether he was pleading the innocence of a someone accused of murder to the Louisiana Supreme Court or preparing for the prosecution of state officials; he was purpose-driven to succeed. If there was a human rights issue, or if an individual was being taken advantage of, Fields persistently attacked. He embraced the Democratic Party and its leaders but was quick to chastise when either would stray from the doctrine that had been adopted by the party or the laws of the nation.

Fields identified himself as being an Independent. In today's definition an Independent would be an individual that is not associated with either the Democratic or Republican Party. Fields was totally devoted to the Democratic Party, but his use of the term *independent* identified that he was free to act according to his own conscience. To truly accomplish this, it takes conviction of cause, standing on the merits of the situation and displaying total integrity.

In 1916, Harvey was elected to the Louisiana senate. In 1921, he successfully campaigned for and won the race for state district attorney. Even though he had been communicating with leaders of the National Democratic Party and was involved with the leadership of the Democratic Party at the local level, it wasn't until 1924 that his potential was being realized. That year, Fields was selected as an alternate to the 1924 Democratic National Convention in New York. He was also completing his four-year period as a Louisiana district attorney, where his conviction rate was an incredible 97 percent.

Fields's attendance at the 1924 convention was without fanfare for the new delegate. He was a member of a delegation that selected its delegate members more by loyalty to leaders of the state party than by affiliation to the party and its platform. Fields studied the workings of the convention and was excited by the atmosphere that surrounded the entire process. He became friends with William Jennings Bryan, a vibrant speaker that had been nominated for president on several occasions. In 1924, Bryan was selected to become the party's vice presidential candidate.

· Seating List ·

THE CITY *of* NEW YORK

DINNER

TO THE

DELEGATES AND ALTERNATES

TO THE

DEMOCRATIC NATIONAL CONVENTION

MONDAY, JUNE TWENTY-THIRD, NINETEEN TWENTY-FOUR

SEVEN P.M.

HOTEL COMMODORE

PERSHING SQUARE AND FORTY-SECOND STREET

MAYOR'S COMMITTEE ON RECEPTIONS
TO DISTINGUISHED GUESTS

HONORABLE JOHN F. HYLAN
The Mayor and Honorary Chairman

RODMAN WANAMAKER
Chairman

GROVER A. WHALEN
Presiding Vice-Chairman

JOHN T. SHERRITT
Secretary

The opening night of the convention was scheduled for the banquet that was hosted by the City of New York. Fields attended and was seated at table 27. This was probably the only event of the convention that displayed a civil tone.

The convention itself was a rowdy event. Roman Catholic delegates would stand in the corridors of the hotels demanding that the Ku Klux Klan be denounced by the Democratic National Convention. William Jennings Bryan fought to keep the Klan issue out of the convention. When he went on the floor to speak of the convention, he was horribly jeered at by the Tammany Hall forces from New York, and it took thirty minutes before he could utter the first word of his speech. Tammany Hall was the New York political leadership headquartered in New York City. Ultimately, the proposition to denounce the Klan failed by seven votes; however, this did identify changes that were going on within the party.

This convention displayed the deep divisions within the Democratic Party. Today's political conventions are tamed events when compared to the 1924 convention. Modern conventions usually select the presidential candidate on the first ballot. When the first ballot of 1924 was cast, the leader was William McAdoo. Al Smith of New York was second. Seventeen other candidates also received votes. By the time the fifteenth ballot was cast, the convention was being referred to as the "Klanbake" due to the chaos from the issue of the Ku Klux Klan. It was noted that possibly 25 percent of the delegates were members of the Klan. After fifteen days and one hundred ballots, the convention was no longer the glamorous affair that it began as. Delegates had run out of money and were telegraphing for funds to pay for their howtel rooms. Everyone was exhausted, and New York was hot in July. Smith had taken the lead in delegate votes at the one-hundred-ballot count, but his Catholic religion made it a sure thing that he could not be elected. McAdoo's support of the Klan doomed his chances. Finally, on the one hundred and third ballot, compromise candidate John Davis won the nomination. After sixteen grueling days, the Democrats had a candidate.

In the 1920s and 30s it was mandatory that a politician have almost superhuman strength and stamina. Several correspondences exist that note that Fields was famous for his stamina and fire-in-the-gut enthusiasm. Huey Long was noted for this as was William Gibbs McAdoo. McAdoo knew Fields through the conventions plus they had a mutual friend with William Jennings Bryan. Bryan not only served as a leader of the Democratic Party but both he and McAdoo served on Woodrow Wilson's cabinet. McAdoo married Wilson's daughter and at the age of seventy-one they divorced at which time he married his twenty-four year old third wife.

Fields was exhilarated. He was known for his energy and enthusiasm throughout his life, and this event was the excitement he craved. He used the 1924 convention to meet individuals from across the country, understand their politics, and engage in discussion about the party. He had a keen desire to know the delegates and was very sociable. One of these acquaintances, James "Jim" Farley became both a lifelong friend of Fields's and the leader of the Democratic Party. Fields also studied the workings of the party, and especially the working of the convention itself.

In 1924, another politician was learning what it was like to be defeated, how to learn from his mistakes, and how to quickly rebound from a loss. Huey Pierce Long had run for governor of Louisiana and lost. Some say the Klan issue, which he refused to address, was his downfall. Long claimed the rain and muddy roads kept his voters from the polls. He did maintain his six-year elected position on the Louisiana Public Service Commission.

A year later, Fields had completed his successful term as district attorney. He left office in 1925 with his 97 percent conviction rate and became chairman of the Louisiana Democratic State Central Committee. It was in 1925 that he received word that a legal duel was about to take place, and he was not to be denied the opportunity to witness it. In the summer of 1925, Harvey traveled to Tennessee, over five hundred miles of dirt roads in the middle of summer, to watch two friends debate a highly contested issue.

Tennessee had passed a bill known as the Butler Act. This act stated that it was a violation in any state-funded education institution in Tennessee to "teach any theory that denies the story of the Divine Creation of man as taught in the Bible, and to teach instead that man descended from a lower order of animals." In other words, evolution, the natural selection of species, and Darwinism was off-limits to the education institutions of Tennessee.

The American Civil Liberties Union (ACLU) announced that it would defend anyone accused of teaching the theory of evolution in defiance of the Butler Act. This offer laid the foundation for what was to become one of the most heralded and famous legal cases in U.S. history. In fact, it began as a major publicity contrivance.

George Rappleyea managed several mines near the town of Dayton, Tennessee. Rappleyea hatched a publicity plan that would draw public attention to this small Tennessee community. He discussed his idea at a local pharmacy with several local businessmen, and following their acceptance, he began executing the plot.

Clark County's high school football coach was John Scopes. Rappleyea approached Scopes and asked him to become a participant in his plot. It had been recognized that the coach had recently taught a biology class when he had substituted for the absent biology teacher and school principal. Rappleyea noted that the state required the teachers to use a specific textbook in the classroom. *Civic Biology* was this book, and it vividly explained evolution and provided the text to teach from.

Scopes not only accepted the assignment, he embraced it with enthusiasm. He incriminated himself even though he wasn't sure that he actually taught the theory. Scopes urged students to testify against him. Judge Raulston did everything he could to get the jury to indict Scopes, short of directly instructing the grand jury to do so. On April 24, John Scopes was indicted on charges of violating the Butler Act by teaching evolution in Dayton, Tennessee. The publicity stunt was moving forward, but no one realized the impact the trial would have.

Two local attorneys would prosecute Scopes. This wasn't good enough for Rappleyea. He contacted H. G. Wells, famous author known for books such as *War of the Worlds*, and asked that he be on the defense team. Wells quickly rebuked the offer. William Riley, founder of the World Christian Fundamentals Association, contacted Fields's friend William Jennings Bryan and asked him to join the prosecution team. Bryan accepted the offer, and the frenzy of the press was on. Clarence Darrow jumped to the challenge and volunteered to join the defense. Fields knew Darrow through his legal profession.

The world converged on small Dayton, Tennessee. The *Baltimore Sun* assisted with the defense expenses. The paper had previously paid the bail of Scopes when he was first arrested. Radio station WGN from Chicago showed up to broadcast the trial. The trial made history as the first United States trial to be broadcast live. Reporters from around the globe were on hand to watch the legal spectacle. Tom Igoe was one of these reporters. He had previously covered the 1924 convention and was now present for the infamous trial.

Fields arrived and visited with the two famous participants. One he knew from politics and one he knew from the study of law. It had been less than a year since he was associated with his friend Bryan at the 1924 convention.

Fields's political friend was William Jennings Bryan. Unfortunately for Bryan, he hadn't tried a case in thirty-seven years, and Darrow would take advantage of it. Bryan was now in his later years of life, but what an exciting life he had led. He was the Democratic candidate for president three times. When Fields was at the marathon sessions of the 1924 convention, Bryan became the candidate for vice president. Even though the country rejected him as president, the country did accept many of his reform doctrines. These included a graduated income tax, women suffrage, Prohibition, federal insurance of bank deposits, stock market regulations, and pure food and drug laws, among others. He remained active in the Democratic Party throughout his life. In 1912, he helped Woodrow Wilson gain the presidential nomination. Wilson rewarded Bryan by naming him secretary of state. In 1915, Bryan resigned his position due to Wilson's movement away from neutrality following the sinking of the *Lusitania*. Once a leader of the Democratic Party, Bryan had lost most of his political clout by the 1924 convention when he backed McAdoo for the nomination.

Bryan was noted for his oratory ability. This served him well with both his law practice and his political career. He is reported to have given twelve speeches in fifteen hours. He would average four one-hour-long speeches a day and punctuated that religion was the foundation of morality.

In 1905, Bryan provided a dire warning in one of his speeches when he stated, "The Darwinian theory represents man reaching his present perfection by the operation of the law of hate—the merciless law by which perfection by which the strong crowd out and kill off the weak. If his is the law of our development then, if there is any logic that can bind the human mind, we shall turn backward to the beast in proportion as we substitute the law of love. I choose to believe that love rather than hatred is the law of development."

In addition to his ability to speak, Bryan had another asset that would prove to be invaluable throughout his career. His wife was fully supportive of him in many ways. They had met when he was a high school teacher and at the same time attending law school, and she was his pupil. Following their marriage and the birth of their first child, Bryan's wife attended law school, graduated, and passed the bar. Her only motive was to support Bryan as she had no desire to actively practice the profession. Together they made a team that would contribute to the United States' political landscape for thirty-five years.

Bryan had a staunch religious upbringing. As a child, he would attend Methodist services in the morning and Baptist services in the afternoon. This formed his deep conviction in the teachings of the Bible and Christian doctrines. He claimed that the most important day of his life was the day he was baptized. Bryan would eventually become a member of the Presbyterian Church, and this would become his dominant denomination.

He studied law in Chicago and moved to Omaha, Nebraska, to practice. In 1892, he was elected to Congress. In 1896, at the age of thirty-six, Bryan became the youngest presidential candidate following his nomination at the convention. He still holds this distinction in political history. During the Spanish-American war, he volunteered for service and became a colonel of a Nebraska militia. This would appear to be a contradiction of the tenets taught by his staunch Christian beliefs. Bryan defended this by stating that universal peace cannot come without justice. This is in line with the writings of John Locke, a 1700s writer whose writings were rumored to have been studied by Thomas Jefferson.

Bryan's fervent belief in creationism, political clout, and his ability to deliver an effective verbal message, plus his immense energy, made him the perfect prosecutor to attack the teachings of Darwinism in public school and the teacher John Scopes.

On the other side of the Scopes Trial was Clarence Darrow. Darrow was Fields's legal profession friend

Darrow was immensely famous for his legal prowess. He was a leader in the ACLU, and since he would have been supporting the side of the oppressed, he would have found a friend in Fields. Darrow would have been a role model for Fields to look up to. His fight for the rights of everyone was instilled in him as a child. His father was an abolitionist, and his mother was an active women's right advocate.

One attribute that both Fields and Darrow possessed was that they placed civil rights above personal wealth or gains. In 1894, Darrow was a corporate lawyer for a railroad company. That year he represented Eugene Debs, head of the American Railway Union, when the union went on strike. In order to provide his defense, Darrow resigned his position as the corporate lawyer for the railroad he represented, thus incurring a major negative impact on his personal income. Fields likewise was respected by the railroad workers, and he was encouraged to continue his support of the railroad workers while he was chairman of the Louisiana Public Service Commission. A copy of one of these letters follows.

C. Y. BOTVIDSON
GENERAL CHAIRMAN
DALLAS, TEXAS
WESTBROOK, TEXAS

A. Y. GARNER
LOCAL CHAIRMAN
TIOGA, TEXAS

W. H. ROBINSON
GEN'L SECRETARY AND TREASURER
BOYCE, LA

The Order of Railroad Telegraphers

TEXAS & PACIFIC SYSTEM, DIVISION No. 88

AFFILIATED WITH
THE AMERICAN FEDERATION OF LABOR

IN YOUR REPLY PLEASE REFER TO FILE

PERSONAL

Boyce La July 9,1935

Hon Harvey G Fields,
Farmerville,La.
Dear Commissioner Fields:-

        News-paper reports indicate that you will
have opposition at the next election.

If I can be of any service to you just call on me at any time
for you know that I am very much interested in keeping Jobs for
all our men and appreciate anything that you do in that direction
at this time when so many are out of employment and needs work so
bad to support their families.

        With very best wishes and kindest personal regards.

        Yours truly,

        W H Robinson

Darrow's first murder case was in 1895, and with the successful defense of Patrick Eugene Prendergast in a well-known murder trial, he was entrenched as a very resourceful trial lawyer. His defense was sensational. He continually took on difficult cases that displayed his legal abilities before the jury, a desire to defend the downtrodden and a burning desire to win his case. His defense of Dr. Ossian Sweet, an African American charged with the murder of a white man in Detroit, has been identified as a landmark in the civil rights movement. Darrow ultimately won the release of all defendants who were initially tried before an all-white jury.

By 1925, Darrow had made a decision to retire following his defense of Leopold and Loeb in the Bobby Franks murder case. Then John Scopes was indicted. Darrow would not be denied the opportunity to be an active participant in what was being billed as one of the highest-profile cases in America, and one that would be covered by the press from around the world. The notoriety associated with the trial plus the fact that Darrow was an agnostic combined to appeal to his internal drive. This was a case designed for Clarence Darrow.

By mid-July, Fields was in Dayton, Tennessee, and the trial was beginning. The ACLU based its defense on the premise that the Butler Act violated Scopes's constitutional rights and was thus unconstitutional. Darrow and the defense team began to change as the trial progressed. The defense began to argue that there really was no conflict between Darwin's evolution theory and the Bible's creationism theory.

The defense team brought in a Johns Hopkins University professor to testify as an expert witness. Seven other expert witnesses were standing by to testify. The judge would only allow written statements, which led to an outburst by Darrow. This caused Darrow to apologize to the judge to prevent a contempt of court against him. The passion of the trial was what everyone was hoping for.

As the trial progressed, Darrow began attacking Bryan's knowledge of other religions, as well as his knowledge of science. Darrow also attacked the literal interpretation of the Bible. In Bryan's major speech of the trial, he used excerpts of Darrow's defense that was used in the Leopold and Loeb case. This would set the tone for the remainder of the trial.

By day 7 of the trial, the proceedings were everything that it was built up to be. Then the trial took an unprecedented twist that took the Scopes Monkey Trial to an even higher level of excitement. Clarence Darrow called William Jennings Bryan to the stand as a witness to demonstrate that the teachings of the Bible in relation to its reference to miracles was unreasonable. Some claim that the call to the stand was spontaneous; however, it is generally agreed that Darrow diligently prepared for the cross-examination the night before.

Two oratorical giants of immense ability faced each other.

Mid-July in Tennessee is hot and humid. Judge Raulston ordered the trial out of doors, and the confrontation began. Darrow attacked Bryan on questions of how Eve could come from Adam's rib, and where did Cain get his wife? Bryan snapped that Darrow could go hunt for her.

Darrow proclaimed, "You insult every man of science and learning in the world because he does not believe in your fool religion."

Bryan shot back, "The reason I am answering is not for the benefit of the superior court. It is to keep these gentlemen from saying I was afraid to meet them and let them question me, and I want the Christian world to know that any atheist, agnostic, unbeliever can question me anytime as to my belief in God, and I will answer him."

Stewart, a member of the prosecution team, asked what the purpose of Darrow's questioning was. Bryan added that it was to "cast ridicule on everybody who believes in the Bible."

After several angry exchanges, Judge Raulston had enough; and after two hours, the examination of Bryan was over. The judge said that nothing was being accomplished and ruled that there would be no cross-examination of Darrow the next day. The world was denied what would have been an undeniable cross-examination of historic proportions.

That night Fields visited with Darrow. He questioned what he was doing to "old man Bryan." Darrow told Fields to stay out of this. He could handle Bryan, but Fields would present a problem. Fields then asked about the merits of the examination and what he was trying to prove. Darrow said he wanted Bryan to admit that Jesus came from one parent. Darrow's agnostic views would have then led him to ask how this could have been biologically possible.

Fields asked him what would happen after he admitted that.

"Then the trial is over," Darrow said.

"Then you have perpetuated an unholy farce on the people of this country," Fields said.

The next day, Darrow declined a summation of the jury. In Tennessee, if the defense does not provide a summation, the prosecutor is not allowed to provide the final argument. Without a summation, the case went to the jury.

It took the jury just nine minutes to reach a verdict of guilty. This was later overturned by the Tennessee Supreme Court over a technicality, and thus, one of the most publicized trials was over. Five days later, William Jennings Bryan ate a large lunch, lay down for a nap, and died.

Fields returned to Farmerville and began both his private practice and his service as the chairman of the Louisiana Democratic State Central Committee. Between 1925 and 1928, Fields joined the law firm that would be known as Long, Fields, and O'Neal. Members of the firm were Huey Pierce Long, Earl K. Long, Robert O'Neal, and Harvey G. Fields.

In 1928, Huey Long was elected governor of Louisiana. At the time of the election, he still had two years remaining on his position of being a member of the Louisiana Public Service Commission. Long had to decide on who his successor would be.

CHAPTER 2

THE EARLY LONG YEARS

F ields was a crusader for the laboring class of Louisiana and America. He disliked arrogance and the way the privileged few used the laborers in the fields and mills. His concern for providing a better life for Louisiana would make him an ideal candidate for leadership in what was about to happen to his native state and the country as a whole.

In 1927, Huey Long was an elected member of the Louisiana Public Service Commission. He had lost the 1924 governor's race but was undaunted. In 1928, Long took over the role as the top executive of Louisiana when he won the gubernatorial election, moved into the governor's mansion when Governor Fuqua's replacement moved out.

Fuqua had died of a massive heart attack while in office and was replaced by his lieutenant governor Ormel Simpson. *Time* magazine was not complementary of Huey at the time of his election as they referred to the newcomer to the national scene as "*a talkative, curly-headed bantamweight on the Public Service Commission*". *Time* also stated that elections in Louisiana are won and lost in the news papers. Huey had already understood the power of the press and would continue to use it as a tactical tool as he grew in political stature.

Fields had been the chairman of the Louisiana Democratic State Central Committee and had also become a member of the Long, Fields, and O'Neal law firm. When Long took office as governor, he would need a replacement for his unexpired term on the Public Service Commission. He didn't look far and selected his friend Harvey Fields. This was a true win-win situation. Long had an ally on the commission, Fields received a position that would allow him to grow, and Louisiana inherited an idealist that would work tirelessly for the farmers and laborers of the state. But who was this man Long that had mesmerized a state and whose popularity was spreading across the country?

Huey Long was born in the rural North Louisiana town of Winnfield in Winn Paris. He was brought up in a large farming family that totaled nine children. Among the family members, brother George became a dentist, and another, brother Earl, became a lawyer and politician. Huey was an excellent student in high school and was noted for his photographic memory.

His brazen attitude that was linked to causes he believed in was recognized at an early age. While in high school in 1908, he circulated a petition to have the principal of Winn Parish schools removed. Long was promptly expelled.

In his senior year, Long won a debating scholarship to LSU. He could not afford the textbooks he would need at LSU, so he was unable to attend the school of his dreams. This unfortunate incident forged a very important piece of his legislation in later years that benefited thousands of underprivileged children.

Since Huey was unable to find the financial means for college, he left home to become a salesman. In 1913, Rose McConnell had won a baking contest that had been sponsored by a poplar vegetable shortening called Cottolene. Long was promoting the product, met Rose, and they were married that year. The marriage lasted until Long's death and produced three children. One son, Russell, later became a dominant force in the United States Senate.

During World War I, Huey's sales jobs began to dry up. He decided that he would enter Oklahoma Baptist University and pursue a career in the ministry. At the same time, Huey's brother George was setting up his dentistry practice in Oklahoma. George allowed Huey to live with him in Shawnee and helped him as much as he could with his living requirements. Huey quickly lost interest, and instead of studying the ministry, he spent most of his time preparing posters and helping a local politician in a political race. The seeds of his political life had been sown.

After leaving the ministry, Long entered the University of Oklahoma law school. This too was short-lived, and he left for Louisiana and ultimately went to Tulane University Law School. After only one year in school, Long requested that the Louisiana board allow him to sit for the bar exam. He finally convinced the board that he was ready, and he sat for and passed the exam. In 1915, Huey moved back to Winnfield and began private practice.

Long later moved to Shreveport, where he spent ten years practicing law and enjoying it, stating that he never took a case against a poor man. In 1918, he was elected to the Louisiana Railroad Commission. This was renamed as the Louisiana Pubic Service Commission in 1921. His main platform during the 1918 campaign was his anti-Standard Oil crusade. When practicing law, he was famous for representing small plaintiffs against big business. Many of these cases involved workmen's compensation cases. His big win was his case against Standard Oil, when he sued them for unfair business practices. This fight would continue throughout his political career. Huey was convinced that Standard Oil was exploiting the state's oil and gas natural resources.

Long successfully used techniques in his 1918 election that would serve him well for the rest of his career. He would attack his opponents unmercifully, used printed circulars, hung large quantities of posters, and traveled the state, providing marathon sessions of speeches.

While serving on the Public Service Commission, he would fight rate increases, pipeline monopolies, and the infamous Standard Oil. His fighting for the rights of the working class made him the perfect candidate as a protégé of Harvey Fields.

In 1924, when Long was running for governor, Fields was attending the Democratic National Convention in New York. That year, Long was defeated in the race for governor but was reelected to the Public Service Commission. Not only did Long have problems with Standard Oil and how he perceived the way they were conducting business in Louisiana, Long was also at odds with the political bosses of New Orleans known as the Old Regulars. This group that formed the backbone of the Democratic Party operated a political machine that controlled the majority of the state. Fortunately for Huey, they only saw him as a minor threat and didn't take him seriously.

Between 1924 and 1928, both Fields and Long were active in their respective endeavors. Long was the chairman of the Louisiana Public Service Commission. Fields completed his duties as district attorney in 1925, following a very successful four-year term.

Harvey Fields had a burning desire to help the oppressed. Fields did not like arrogance, and he felt that each man deserved equal respect. He also believed that elected officials should support and provide for the constituents that they represented. In 1927, Fields took on Riley Wilson. Not only did Wilson represent the qualities that Fields disliked, he was also running for governor against Long. The following news release was prepared by Fields as an attack on Wilson. This feud would last for many years of Fields's career. Fields viewed Wilson as a man who abandoned the labor class of Louisiana.

FIELDS CHARGES WILSON UNFRIENDLY TO LABOR.

Farmerville, Louisiana
September 10th, 1937.

H. G. Fields, Chairman of the State Democratic Central Committee
of Louisiana, former sponsor for the O. R. C. Organization when it
made its famous fight in the Louisiana Legislature, in a discussion
relating to Riley J. Wilson's labor record said to-day:

Mr. Wilson has been opposed to the most prominent labor move-
ments and legislation ever before Congress. He stated Saturday before
opening the Long meeting at Farmerville, as temporary chairman, to a
number of the Long people while in conference and later to Mr. Long,
Mr. Cyr and others, after the meeting, that he was prepared to show
that Mr. Wilson had not been friendly to the Labor Unions or in
sympathy with the labor people at the time they needed him most, and
having been asked to make good his charge submitted the following facts:

In 1919 or 1920 I was approached by Mr. Tom Greer, former
President of Louisiana Federation of Labor, a close friend of mine, and
asked if some of Mr. Wilson friends could not prevail upon him to be
more friendly to labor, and at the same time Mr. Greer charged that
Mr. Wilson had not been friendly to labor and cited several noted
instances, and thereafter I investigated the question myself and
these are the disclosures.

1st.   In 1916 when the Nolan Bill, before Congress for a minimum wage
to Government Employees, was up for consideration Wilson opposed the
matter and was unfavorable to labor.

2nd.   When the Lunn Amendment War Material Labor bill was before
Congress in March 1918 Wilson did not show up and the records placed
him in what is known as the "Ducking Class".

3rd.   In January 1919 he took an unfavorable position to the Federal
Employee Bonus Bill, which was for the benefit of the poor, underpaid
servants and employees of the Government, but fought to raise his
salary as a Congressman.

4th.   In the 66th Congress when the Nolan Minimum Wage Bill was
again before Congress Wilson was found on the negative side.

5th.-- Worst of all in October 1919 when the Vocational Rehabilitation
Bill for poor, cripples and unfortunates was up before Congress,
Wilson turned a deaf ear and was found on the unfavorable side.

6th.   When the final passage of the Civil Service Retirement Bill
for poor and aged employees came up, backed by the Labor Unions,
Riley Wilson was found on the negative side of the fence.

7th.   In 1922 when the important Immigration Measure in which labor
was interested came before the house, he again joined the "Ducking Class".

8th.   In April, 1924 when the Child Labor Amendment Law came before
Congress, backed by the Labor Unions, backed by many women leaders
of the country, Wilson was found again on the negative side of the fence.

9th.   When the Howell-Barkley Railroad Bill came up Wilson for the
third time joined the Ducking Class and marked not present.

Four times he was not present, did not answer when important
labor measures were before Congress. Six times he voted against the
most important labor bills and once he paired unfavorable to labor.

Now I leave the public to decide whether Wilson has been a
friend to labor. I can see now why it is a great many of the labor
leaders, one by one, are falling in line with Long, the friend of
labor and the Champion of the cause of the people.

(signed)
H. G. Fields

LAW OFFICES OF

LONG, FIELDS & O'NEAL

NINTH FLOOR CITY BANK BLDG.

SHREVEPORT, LOUISIANA

HUEY P. LONG
EARL K. LONG
HARVEY G. FIELDS
ROBT. J. O'NEAL

NO PRACTICE ACCEPTED WITH OR
BEFORE ANY STATE DEPARTMENT

The firm consisted of Huey, his brother Earl, Fields, and Robert O'Neal. Each would carve out a successful career in Louisiana law and politics. Though this was listed as a partnership, there was no misunderstanding that Huey was the senior partner and the other members were equal junior partners.

By 1928, Huey was wearing his trademark white suits. This suited him well when he strolled into the courtroom in defense of some downtrodden citizen that Huey felt was being taken advantage of by big business.

In one case, Long and Fields successfully took a case to the United States Court of Appeals, where they were appealing a ruling that favored Transcontinental Oil Company. In this case, the courts ruled against Mrs. Ethel Thomas, who alleged that the oil company had taken advantage of her. It was a perfect case for the law firm to accept—it met the social requirements that Huey practiced under—and in 1928, they argued the original ruling to the court of appeals.

IN THE

UNITED STATES CIRCUIT COURT OF APPEALS

FIFTH CIRCUIT

No. 5368

TRANSCONTINENTAL OIL COMPANY,
Appellant and Plaintiff in Error,

versus

MRS. ETHEL THOMAS, ET AL.,
Appellees and Defendants in Error.

APPLICATION FOR REHEARING.

HUEY P. LONG,
HARVEY GOODWYN FIELDS,
ROBERT J. O'NEAL,
EARL K. LONG,
LONG, FIELDS & O'NEAL,
Attorneys for Appellees, Defendants
in Error.

MONTGOMERY-ANDREE PRINTING CO. INC. 430-432 CHARTRES, N.O.

By the time the 1928 elections were held, Long had solidified his position with Louisiana voters. He had gone to the masses of rural Louisianans that had been disenfranchised by the Old Regulars. With Louisiana having the highest illiteracy rate in the nation—no free textbooks and fewer than three hundred miles of paved roads—Long painted a picture of hope for the oppressed. He also crossed the sacred religious boundary, appealed to both Catholic and Protestant voters and thus consolidated voters in the Protestant North with the voters of the Catholic South.

Long adopted the phrase "Every man a king, but no one wears a crown." This was a phrase first used by Fields's friend and presidential candidate William Jennings Bryan. The phrase, coupled with Long's message and his new campaign techniques, served him well. He won the 1928 election by the largest margin in Louisiana history. Coming in second was Congressman Riley Wilson.

Huey Long now had a decision to make. He would have to select his own replacement for the Louisiana Public Service Commission. This person would have to be both loyal to Long and would have to be a staunch fighter for the causes that Long had championed. Who better to select than Harvey G. Fields? The press coverage in the New Orleans *Times-Picayune* pertaining to the selection of Fields for Public Service Commissioner follows.

FIELDS WILL FILL LONG'S UNEXPIRED COMMISSION TERM
Governor Appoints Partner to Public Service Post

Baton Rouge, La. Aug 7. Harvey G. Fields of Farmerville, law partner of Governor Huey P. Long, was appointed a member of the Louisiana Public Service Commission today to fill the vacancy created when Mr. Long became governor May 21st.

Mr. Fields was commissioned for the unexpired term of Governor Long which ends in 1930. Mr. Long was re-elected a member of the commission in 1924 for a six year term. The other members of the Public Service Commission are: Francis Williams of New Orleans, chairman, and Dudley J. LeBlanc of Lafayette, vice chairman.

Shortly after Governor Long took office he received an opinion from the attorney-general to the effect that the governor is authorized to appoint members of the Public Service Commission when vacancies occur, irrespective of the time the terms have to run.

Governor Long, after receiving the opinion, announced that he intended appointing George Wesley Smith of Rayville, Richland parish. When Mr. Smith became associated with the defense of Major Frank T. Payne, former chairman of the Louisiana Highway Commission, he wrote Governor Long saying that he wished to withdraw his name for consideration for the appointment.

Mr. Fields has held a number of political offices, including that of state senator. He is chairman of the Fifth Congressional District Democratic Executive Committee and is a former chairman of the Democratic Central Committee. He was chosen by the central committee as an alternate to Governor Long to the Democratic National Convention in Houston and in the absence of Governor Long he served as a delegate. He was a member of the credentials committee, and was chosen by the Louisiana delegation to direct the defense of it when its' credentials were attacked.

Mr. Fields several months ago became associated as the law partner of Governor Long, the firm known as Long, Fields and O'Neal, maintaining offices in Shreveport and Farmerville, Union Parish.

One member of the Long, Fields, O'Neal law firm was every bit as controversial as Huey. Earl, brother of Huey, became a household name in the 1950s while serving as governor of Louisiana. But before he was nicknamed the "crazy governor," Earl was better known a Huey's little brother.

Earl was born in 1895 in Winnfield. His brother Huey was not the only politician in the family. Brother George, dentist and early ministry supporter of Huey, was elected as a U.S. representative. Also, his sister's son, John Hunt, would eventually obtain the position of chairman of the Public Service Commission. That is the same position held by both Huey Long and Harvey Fields.

Fields and Earl had very little personal contact outside the law firm. Fields never referenced Earl in his political correspondence, and he never called on Earl for support.

In 1932, Earl ran for lieutenant governor. Brother Huey wouldn't support him but instead endorsed John Fournet. Fournet, who won the contest, later became chief justice of the Louisiana Supreme Court. The remainder of the family supported Earl, but Huey held the dominant power. Earl was enraged.

Earl blasted Huey by referring to him as "the yellowest physical coward that God has ever let live."

Huey responded with, "Earl is my brother, you know, but he's crooked. If you live long enough, he'll double-cross you. He'd double-cross Jesus Christ if he was down here on earth." Eight years later, when referring to Richard Leche, Earl would comment about Jesus being double-crossed by one of his disciples. In 1941, Fields would witness firsthand Huey's prophetic statement about Earl come true.

The feud between Huey and Earl would be a continual source of sensationalism for the newspapers. One confrontation took place during a commission meeting that was investigating Huey. Roosevelt had embarked on a campaign to discredit Long and had launched an investigation into Long's involvement in the election of Senator John H. Overton. In fact, Fields commented in one letter that he had been a campaign manager of Overton's successful bid for the Senate. At the hearing, Earl was providing information that was detrimental to Huey. A copy of the picture that appeared in Louisiana papers showing the committee follows:

'Lie,' Says Senator Long, as Brother Testifies

Earl K. Long (A) and his brother, Senator Huey P. Long (B), had opposing positions before the Senate special investigating committee Tuesday when testimony offered as a witness by Earl Long was described by his brother as a "_____ _____ lie."

Earl did eventually win a number 2 position, and in 1936, he was the lieutenant governor of Louisiana. Little did he know that actions taken by Fields would eventually lead to Long being sworn in as governor of the state.

In 1944, Earl lost his bid to be elected lieutenant governor. Perseverance is a hallmark of the Long family. In 1948, Earl ran for and was elected as the governor of Louisiana. Long defeated the former governor, reformist, and candidate that Fields had supported in 1940—Sam Jones.

Louisiana had a term limit when Earl was running for office. The governor could not be reelected, so Earl was forced to sit out the next race; however, he was back in the running in 1955.

Earl easily won, and the next four years, Louisiana became a media circus for the country. Long had made the statement that "Louisiana would someday elect good government, and they won't like it." Earl also adopted the name *Uncle Earl*, which stuck with him. He took the controversial move of removing voting restrictions for the blacks in the state. Long pushed the move through the state legislature to equalize pay for teachers of both races. This served both the civic responsibility the Long name was famous for and the political strategy they were notorious for. Earl knew that if he freed the black voters in the state to have easy access to the polls, the block vote would go to him.

Earl became the source of numerous national news stories during his last governorship. He was placed in a mental hospital by his wife. He promptly had the head of the state hospital administration fired, and the replacement had him immediately released. One speculation is that Long had been hospitalized due to personal actions of his wife, who was furious over his relationship with a New Orleans stripper. Blaze Starr was another subject of press coverage that spotlighted Louisiana politics and kept Earl in the limelight. Upon his death, Long left Blaze a sizable amount of money. She promptly refused it.

In 1959, Long was unable to run for governor as he was once again term limited. Instead, he would run for lieutenant governor on the ticket of Fields's close friend, James A. Noe. The ticket lost to Jimmy "You Are My Sunshine" Davis, and this ended Noe's political career. Earl Long was undaunted.

In the fall of 1959, Long came to Farmerville and spoke to the populace in the Farmerville courthouse. Loudspeakers were outside, and the hundreds of people that could not get a seat in the courthouse could sit under the massive oak trees and listen to the speech. Absent from the crowd was former law partner Harvey Fields. Long finished his speech and left town without a word to Fields.

In 1960, Long was elected to the U.S. Congress. It is alleged that he was suffering a heart attack on Election Day, but due to fear of negative voter impact, he refused medical help until the polls closed. Several days later, on September 5, 1960, Earl Long, known as the "last of the red hot poppas" died peacefully.

To add to the Long mystique and legend, it is reported that Earl, like his brother Huey, died on the day of an eclipse.

But in 1928, Fields embraced his position as a member of the Public Service Commission. What better position for an activist for the rights of the laboring class than to be in this situation?

CHAPTER 3

A TRAIN RIDE TO HOUSTON

In 1928, Huey Long was governor of Louisiana. He had defeated the bosses of the state, the Old Regulars that had run Louisiana for years. These manipulators of the "common man" were being replaced by a different type of leader that required total control but was viewed by many as a modern-day Robin Hood. Fields had been selected to complete the last two years of Long's term on the Public Service Committee. This served Fields well as he now had a great sense of purpose. The depression was about to begin, and he had an opportunity to help the downtrodden of rural Louisiana.

The conservatives of the state did not like or trust Long, but they did understand that he had the ear of the voters, and they needed to placate him. Long knew that these leaders of the old approach to state leadership would object to many of his programs that were directed to support the populace and not the individual. It was noted in the New Orleans *Morning Tribute* that Long stated in a speech delivered at a party hosted by the conservatives to honor him, "I go into the Governor's office as your servant." Long went on to say, "In no sense of the word as the master of the people or of any set of people."

Items of improvement noted in Long's speech were improved education facilities, attacking illiteracy, better care of the unfortunate, and fairer labor laws. In essence, Long was placing big business and its supporters on notice that a new administration with a new agenda was in office, and the number one agenda item was taking care of the general population of Louisiana.

This was a perfect situation for Fields to be in. He was an idealist that loved the idea of a just cause. Like James Farley in New York, Fields had a phenomenal ability to organize and then manage that organization. Fields was being prepared to be an effective member of the Public Service Commission, the same commission that Long had chaired prior to becoming governor. But there were other more pressing issues required of Fields to help Huey expand his influence over the state and increase his visibility to the nation.

Following Long's election to the governorship of Louisiana, it was time for him to expand his control and begin his dominance over a state that was looking for a champion, someone to take care of the workingman that had long been forgotten.

The next goal to conquer would be one that would help solidify his domination of the state and continue to propel him into the national spotlight.

In the summer of 1928, the Democratic National Convention was scheduled to be held in Houston. Huey was determined that he would have his own set of delegates present and seated at the convention. He realized that it would take a legal pleading that would be tested to its extreme. It was understood that the presentation had to be flawless. Long looked to his close ally, former law partner, and legal genius, Harvey Fields, to develop the plan of attack.

The Louisiana Democratic State Central Committee met in New Orleans. This meeting was held several days after the conservatives held the glorious banquet in honor of Long's election, where he was presented with a chest of silver, and at which time the Old Regulars mistakenly thought they had appeased Huey. The purpose of the Democratic State Central Committee meeting was to plan for a state convention to select delegates to the Democratic National Convention in Houston.

Custom dictated how delegates to the convention would be selected. A slate would be identified. This list of potential members to the delegation was based on a certain quantity of people from each congressional district and a number of at-large candidates. Then the governor and the state and city bosses would endorse the slate. An election would be held to select the delegates, and the few interested voters would elect these members. Also, other delegates were selected by the proportional strength of their party. As the Old Regulars, Long's adversary, had the greatest strength in the process, they would thus have a sizable number of delegates. Huey saw that the Louisiana delegation could turn into either a round of horse trading under no control, or he could see the delegates coming under the control of his enemies. Either of these options would lead to the newly elected governor being viewed as a weak leader in the nation's eyes. Long didn't like this; he wanted the lion's share of power provided by the delegates and thus turned to Fields.

Before the Democratic State Central Committee met to select delegates to the 1928 convention, Huey Long and Harvey Fields had begun an intensive investigation as to how delegates could get chosen for the convention. They wanted to know if there was a method that would benefit Long. The two discovered that the Louisiana constitution recognized delegates that were selected by a convention. They also discovered that even though the constitution recognized the delegates, there was not a constitutional requirement that dictated the selection of the delegates through a convention. The constitution only told of how the process would be executed if a convention was held. Long had what he was looking for. The Democratic State Central Committee had the authority to eliminate the convention requirement and name the delegates itself. Huey decided that he could use the promise of jobs to control the majority of the committee's votes. The one person that could orchestrate this was the chairman of the Democratic State Central Committee. At that time, the chairman of the committee was Harvey G. Fields.

Fields had actually started researching the workings of the Democratic National Convention as it pertains to seating of delegates and the use of the convention's "unit rule" for presidential candidate selection. He started this investigation prior to Long's requirement for assistance. This previous work expedited the understanding of the convention rules, plus it had Louisiana moving in the direction of changes to the Democratic National Convention. So adept was Fields in the processes and rules required to run the National Democratic Party that he was selected as a member of the rules committee of the 1944 Democratic National Convention.

In January of 1927, Fields contacted a prestigious law firm in Jackson, Mississippi, requesting information as to how their delegation was instructed to vote and the use of the unit rule. The head of the law firm that Fields communicated with, W. Calvin Wells, was later elected president of the Mississippi Bar Association in 1934 and was then later inducted as a prestigious fellow of the same organization. The communication to Fields from Wells follows.

WELLS, STEVENS AND JONES

LAWYERS

W. CALVIN WELLS
J. MORGAN STEVENS
L. BARRETT JONES
W. CALVIN WELLS, III

LAMAR LIFE BUILDING

JACKSON, MISSISSIPPI

January 28, 1927.

Hon. H. G. Fields,
Attorney-at-Law
Framerville, La.

Dear Sir:

   Your letter of the 21st instant to
hand and contents noted.

   In recent years, to my recollection,
Mississippi has usually sent its delegates
to National Conventions uninstructed but they
usually vote by direction under the unit rule.

        Very truly yours,

WCW-S
1263.

Fields also contacted the governor of Arkansas and requested information on the instructions to delegates. Response to Fields's letter was addressed to the chairman of the Democratic State Central Committee. This identified Fields as the leader of the organization, which ultimately selected the Long slate for the 1928 Democratic National Convention.

The letter below identifies John E. Martineau as the governor of Arkansas. Martineau was in office as a governor for only two years but was noted as a man of integrity who demonstrated innovative change in source funding, and the man who launched the Arkansas highway system. A common thread was developing between the goals of the Long administration and the leaders that Fields was associated with. Like Martineau, the Long administration was driven to provide roads, bridges, and better transportation for the state.

JOHN E. MARTINEAU
GOVERNOR

STATE OF ARKANSAS
EXECUTIVE CHAMBER
LITTLE ROCK

January 25, 1927

J. H. SCHNEIDER
SECRETARY

Hon. H. G. Fields, Chairman,

   State Democratic Central Committee,

      Farmerville, La.

Dear Mr. Fields:

      In reply to your inquiry of
the 21st inst., the Governor directs me to
advise you that we have no hard and fast rule
in this State with reference to instructing
our delegates to the Democratic National Convention. Ordinarily, however, the delegates
go uninstructed.

      Trusting that this is the in-
formation you desire, I remain,

              Yours very truly,

              Jos H. Schneider

              Private Secretary.

Charles Hillman Brough was the twenty-fifth governor of Arkansas. He is recognized as one of the best governors to have held the office in the state. Brough was extremely intelligent and ultimately received a PhD from Johns Hopkins University. He was noted for his speaking abilities, and even filled Baptist pulpits on Sundays. Like James Farley in New York, Brough would look outside the box to develop his political strategy.

Brough had kept records of students he taught at the University of Arkansas and the numerous civic club members that had heard him speak. This would serve as his core support group when he needed political assistance, and he used it to his advantage.

During the gubernatorial election that placed Brough in the governor's mansion, race played a part of the dialogue. Candidate and secretary of state Earle Hodges promised that whites would determine where the African Americans would live. Another candidate, Lewis Smith, promised "a cake of corn bead and a pint of potlicker." Brough was also attacked on allegedly promoting race mixing due to Brough authoring a book on Utah and linking him to the Mormon religion. In the end, Brough won the state by a landslide and served from 1917 to 1921.

Brough proved to be a progressive leader, and many consider him to be the most progressive governor Arkansas has ever seen. Like Long, Brough realized the importance of providing education to the populace, and he enacted legislation for more money for education, plus a compulsory school attendance law, vocational education, and the creation of a state commission of charities and corrections. Brough's administration also supported the strengthening of the state's Prohibition laws and led the South on women's rights.

Following his leaving office, Brough became a lecturer and a publicity agent for the Arkansas Advancement Association. It was this position he was holding when Fields requested information about how Arkansas seated its Democratic National Convention delegates. It is interesting to note that Brough eventually opposed the attempt to prevent Baptists in the state from voting for Catholic Al Smith following the 1928 convention. He also raised the ire of the Baptist State Convention when he opposed banning the teachings of Charles Darwin and evolution in the Arkansas schools. This was the same issue that launched the Scopes Monkey Trial in Tennessee.

In 1927, Fields communicated with Brough. A copy of the letter from Brough to Fields relating to the Democratic National Convention follows:

Arkansas Public Service Information Bureau
Little Rock, Arkansas.

CHARLES H. BROUGH
DIRECTOR

January 25, 1927

PUBLISHERS OF
"ARKANSAS UTILITY NEWS"

"THAT THE PUBLIC MAY BE BETTER INFORMED"

Hon. E. C. Fields
Farmersville, Louisiana

My dear Mr. Fields:

Upon my return from Shreveport I found your good letter of the 22nd instant. I heartily congratulate the Democratic Party of Louisiana upon your election to Chairmanship of the State Democratic Central Committee.

Answering your question with reference to the present Unit Rule, I favor the abolition of the Unit Rule in the event the Two-third Rule is abolished. My experience in two Democratic National Conventions has lead me to the belief that the Two-third Rule is a political anachronism and should be abolished. The abolition of the Unit Rule would insure a more indefinite type of proceedure.

I regret that I will be in Hot Springs this week and, therefore, will not have the pleasure of seeing you personally, so I am writing you with reference to my views on this subject.

Very cordially your friend,

Former Governor of Arkansas

CHB-b

The two-thirds rule was changed at the 1936 convention, and the unit rule was eventually eliminated at the 1968 convention.

In 1928, the Louisiana Democratic State Central Committee was called to order on February 18. Following the call to order, a member of the committee offered a resolution, declaring that the committee should select the national delegates in lieu of the old method. The motion was seconded, and Long's supporters quickly voted to enact the new method of delegation selection. Colonel Ewing (Robert Ewing) was selected as the national committeeman, and Long was selected as a delegate at large. Fields had been offered the national committeeman position by Long but declined in favor of Ewing. The selection method caused turmoil in the ranks of the Old Regulars as they did not have one delegate named to the convention.

New Orleans Mayor Arthur J. O'Keefe was beside himself and displayed his displeasure. Huey enjoyed the turmoil caused by this. "No music ever sounded one-half so refreshing as the whines and groans of the pie-eating politicians," Huey declared. The Old Regulars would not go down without a fight, and they proceeded to select their own set of delegates to the convention. A floor fight at the Democratic National Convention in Houston was building. Harry Gamble from New Orleans attacked the Long administration in the New Orleans *Item* for the legal maneuvering that ultimately had the Long delegates selected for the convention. Fields quickly responded to the attack in a most eloquent press release to the same paper. That release follows:

FIELDS REPLIES TO GAMBLE.

H.G.Fields, former Chairman of the State Democratic Central Committee, and now a Committeeman at Large from the Fifth District replying to the article said to be written by Harry Gamble, and published in the New Orleans Item of February 21st, had the following to say:-

"Mr. Gamble discusses the question of selection of the delegates and of a National Committeeman in a very passionate and rash manner of mind, almost approaching his angry attitude in the Convention Saturday when he espoused the cause of the bosses against the country."

"The State Democratic Central Committee is not a clerical body, it is the organization which governs and controls party affairs in Louisiana, so created by law and by the Statutes of this State. It formulates the rules and proceedure for all other committees, Parish and District, and it has the power to call a Convention, but it is not obliged to do so."

"The resolution that Mr. Gamble sponsored would have given to the fifteen ward leaders (bosses) of New Orleans, who represent the regular organization the power to select delegates without any regard to the desires of a considerable number of the people of New Orleans, just as was done several years ago."

"The State Central Committee, composed of one hundred four Democrats, elected by the people and those at large, selected by the entire Committee, could not accept the resolution sponsored by Mr. Gamble and his associates, and by a vote of two to one repudiated that resolution,and instead,as the party organization vested with the power to do so, and with the approval of the people, selected a National Committeeman and delegates to the next National Convention."

"Mr. Gamble forgets that he did try to throttle down the throats of the democracy of Ascension Parish a defeated candidate, caused the old State Central Committee to be embarrassed by a law suit and at this time it ill behooves him to try to pose as the Leader of Democracy in Louisiana."

"The majority of the people of Louisiana are tickled to death, they want bosses and boss rule abolished and it took the action of a bold and the fearless agent of democracy to do it, and the graceful thing now is for our friend to accept the resolution in the manner of a good sport and a game loser."

Fields had taken on the political bosses of New Orleans and was instrumental in breaking up the boss rule of the time and ultimately allowing rural Louisiana to have a say in the politics of the state. While Louisiana broke with tradition and selected its delegates according to the new Long/Fields method, other states were selecting delegates and committing to candidates prior to the convention. Several states that sent delegates "instructed," directing the delegates whom to vote for, and had selected who the first vote of the convention would be given to. In mid-April, pledges of eighty-six delegates from New York, twelve from Maine, twenty-six from Wisconsin, and thirty from Michigan swelled the committed delegate votes for New York governor Al Smith to a total of 244. Smith's campaign stated that they would have 550 delegates committed by May 15, with a total of 735 required to nominate the presidential candidate. Since Louisiana now sent their delegates uninstructed, not committed to any candidate, the Louisiana delegation was a plum for any candidate.

In June of 1928, the Louisiana delegation would travel by train from New Orleans to Houston. Fields acted as the chairman and kept close contact with Huey. Long had to remain in Baton Rouge to oversee the legislature that was in session.

When Fields and his delegation arrived at the train station, they quickly discovered that other delegations from the East were also on board. Soon after boarding the train, a delegate from New York quickly sought out Fields. The delegate introduced himself as Franklin Delano Roosevelt, and he had a deal for Harvey.

Roosevelt was the presidential campaign manager for New York governor Al Smith. If the Louisiana delegation would support Smith as the Democratic nominee for president, the New York delegation would support Fields and the Long delegation when the debate was held as to which state delegation would be seated. When the train reached Houston, Fields quickly called Long with the proposal and advised that Long accept it. A major concern within the Democratic leadership at the time of the 1928 convention was that Smith was a Catholic. This did not pose a major political obstacle for Long due to Louisiana having a predominately Catholic population in the southern part. Fields was certain that Smith would get the nomination, and it would make sense to align with the Democratic nominee and possibly the future president.

"Damn, a president. I don't care about that. I just want the Huey Long delegation seated. You tell 'em to vote for, Smith," Long said.

The two Democratic delegations presented their credentials, and the Fields-led delegation was voted to be seated. Keeping true to the agreement, Louisiana voted for Al Smith, who ultimately won the Democratic nomination for president. This also solidified a long-standing bond between Fields and James Farley that lasted throughout their lives.

The 1928 convention represented the first Democratic National Convention held in the South since the Civil War. This was not the only first that came from the convention. Smith ultimately received the delegate votes required and became the first Catholic nominated for president. It wouldn't be until John F. Kennedy won the presidential election that a Catholic was placed in the highest position of the land. Another first that came from the election was that Smith was the first Democratic to lose more than one Southern state in the general election.

Conventions held prior to the 1940s were a far cry from their predecessors. A large number of candidates would be presented to the convention for consideration of nomination. Following the first round of votes that certainly never led to a two-thirds majority for any candidate, the horse trading began. It became a marathon of speeches, new votes, and debates. Fights could break out as passions for candidates and their selection of causes swelled to a boiling point. Ultimately, a delegate would be selected.

The original list of candidates presented to the 1928 convention consisted of twenty Democrats from across the country. An additional eleven candidates were vying for the vice president position. Texas was passionately against Smith. After numerous ballots that ultimately saw Smith selected as the presidential candidate, Texas would publicly oppose Smith's anti-Prohibition platform.

One interesting plank of the Democratic National Convention related to the Philippines. This plan called for the independence of the Philippines and noted that the Philippines demonstrated the ability to govern itself. It would take many years and a world war before this was finally realized.

The Democratic Party displayed a progressive approach to another issue of the time. This was the declaration of equality for women in political matters. One woman, Nellie Ross, was listed as a candidate for vice president. She was later a vice chairman of the National Democratic Committee.

Nellie Tayloe Ross was a leader in the Democratic Party and had met Harvey Fields at the 1928 convention. She later became the first female governor in the United States. Ross was also devoutly dedicated to Prohibition, and it appears in the following letter that Harvey had raised questions about the issue. Nellie is concerned that the issue of Prohibition could cause greater cracks in the party. She feels that even though this is a concern, it should be accepted and should not overshadow the more important issues facing the party at that time.

DEMOCRATIC NATIONAL COMMITTEE
NATIONAL PRESS BUILDING
WASHINGTON, D. C.

NELLIE TAYLOE ROSS
VICE-CHAIRMAN

TELEPHONE
NATIONAL 8364

May 11, 1931

Hon. Harvey G. Fields,
Farmerville, La.

My dear Mr. Fields:

     Your letter has too long awaited my acknowledgment but as Miss White wrote you, I have been temporarily indisposed part of the time, and part of the time out on trips since I heard from you.

     It is pleasant to know you remember having met me at the Houston Convention. I agree with you that the Democratic Party has to be "as wise as a serpent and as harmless as a dove" in dealing with certain phases of the situation that now confronts it. The Republican party is so absolutely vulnerable and in such a defensive position that we must keep those facts before the people, and at the same time offer them, in the next campaign, sound, honest policies, formulated upon pure Jeffersonian principles, as a means of relief from the present deplorable economic conditions. As you imply, there is no doubt that our first obligation is to renew allegiance to our Jeffersonian Democracy.

     Now, with reference to the painful problem of prohibition,- for I do assert it is painful to me,- we may as well recognize that we have no choice about its being an issue. It is the people and not party leaders who make issues, and that is a subject on every one's tongue. It is my earnest hope that it shall not be allowed to loom so large as to obscure the tariff question, farm relief, unemployment, water power, and kindred economic problems. You would not, however, I venture to say, have our party dodge or straddle a question that is vital and far-reaching, both in its moral and economic bearing upon the public welfare. It is my opinion that the party in its platform will have to offer some constructive proposal.

     It is my earnest hope that in the year and half between now and the '32 campaign that Democrats will be applying their minds to cool and dispassionate study of the problem with determination that they will not gratify the Republicans by rending the party asunder over it during the campaign, but that the will of the majority shall crystallize into the party platform, and that a united Democracy will stand behind the platform.

     I will say this to you, so seriously do I take the question, that as much as I want the party to win, I am more concerned that it shall do what is right than about the consequences. Never will I champion any policy that I do not think best for society at large.

     I have written you a long letter and yet I am not certain that I have answered the query in your mind. I shall ask that recent speeches and articles I have written be sent you, that you may further consider, if you are interested, what my principles are. I am glad that you wrote me.

Yours most sincerely,

Nellie Tayloe Ross

NTR:W

This letter demonstrates that Fields's idealism is reinforced by the feelings of Ross. It also identifies the plight of America at the time and the issues that faced a country in the middle of the throes of the Great Depression.

After Smith was nominated, he tried to heal the wounds of the party that emulated from his nomination. Smith's acceptance speech was promising for the Democratic Party and stressed that neither geography nor religion nor political influence would have an impact on his administration. This was a speech full of idealistic verbiage with hopes of pulling the Democratic Party together.

Time magazine identified in its July 16, 1928, issue the cracks that formed in the Democratic Party due to Smith's nomination. In the article titled "Bandwagon" the *New York Times* was quoted as publishing, "The first week after a national convention is always devoted to the noble political art of climbing aboard. There ought to be a rule against looking when the ungraceful act is performed."

Louisiana was solidly behind Smith largely due to the desire of Huey Long for it to be so. The other Southern states were not quite as accommodating. Texas governor Dan Moody and Georgia governor L. G. Hardman showed party support and climbed on the bandwagon by simply stating, "I am a Democrat." They did not formally endorse the candidate, only the party. North Carolina's Senator Simmons would not speak against Smith, nor did he say that he would actively support Smith, but did point to his own Democratic record, insinuating that he supported the party.

Some did break with the support of Smith. Senator Heflin of Alabama suggested a new set of Democratic nominees and then vote for these. Thomas Love, a candidate for lieutenant governor of Texas, stated, "As between chronic corruption and acute corruption, I prefer the acute. I want strongly to turn the rascals out, but I am just as strongly opposed to turning Tammany Hall in. I intend to defiantly vote against Smith . . . As long as I live I am going to stay in the Democratic Party."

Smith had an uphill fight ahead of him. His wife was unabashedly blunt when speaking and could alienate women voters. His links to Tammany Hall didn't go well with many Democratic supporters. Even his adoption of "The Streets of New York" as his campaign song had a detrimental affect among rural voters.

In the fall of 1928, the elections were held; and following the normal course of battle from the Republican Party, plus cracks in the Deep South coupled with religious prejudice and associations with Tammany Hall, Al Smith was defeated. News reporter Frederick William Wile stated that Smith lost to the three Ps: Prohibition, Prejudice, and Prosperity. This ended his political career, although he did stay active in the party. He later had a major falling-out with Roosevelt over the New Deal policies. So major was the disconnect that Smith actively supported Republicans in their bid to unseat Roosevelt in the 1936 and 1940 elections.

Eleanor Roosevelt remained close friends with Smith just as she did with James Farley following the Roosevelt/Farley breakup in 1940. Following a bashing of the Roosevelt administration by Smith on a radio program in Washington, Eleanor invited Smith to visit and stay at the White House. He politely declined.

In 1929, Smith became the president of Empire State Inc. The corporation built and then operated the Empire State Building. Interestingly, a supplier of building material for what was then the tallest building in the world was General Builders Corporation, a corporation formed and managed by Smith's former political manager, James Farley.

Although Smith ceased to hold political office, he did publicly speak for issues that he felt were right or against issues that were not in line with his progressive feelings. Fields responded to one of these broadcasts, and Smith was quick to return a response. These letters follow.

August 24th, 1933.

Honorable Alfred E. Smith,
New York City, N. Y.

My Dear Mr. Smith:-

This expresses my heartfelt
commendation upon your splendid address in
favor of the N. R. A., and your position in
coming out so openly and frankly in favor
of the Recovery System, and to the aid of
President Roosevelt.

I still think you are one of
the biggest boys in the party, and that you
are doing a great deal towards holding the
situation well in line.

With best of wishes for your
continued success, and remaining one of your
staunch admirers, I am

Yours very truly,

HGF/hna...

ALFRED E. SMITH.
PRESIDENT

EMPIRE STATE, INC.

NEW YORK.

August 29th, 1933

Honorable Harvey G. Fields,
Farmerville,
Louisiana.

My dear Commissioner:

Thank you for your kind letter of
August twenty-fourth. I am glad to know
that you were so well pleased with the
radio address.

Sincerely yours,

Alfred E. Smith

ses:ccp

By 1933, Fields was chairman of the Public Services Commission and was performing a good job managing and administering this commission. The country was now in the depths of the Great Depression. Prior to the depression, Fields had fought for causes that would improve the lives of rural Louisiana farmers and small-business owners, as well as for the industrial blue-collar workers. With the depression leading to so much anguish and disruption of the family unit across the land, Fields's crusade was ever more important. The National Recovery Administration (NRA) promised to be one solution, where the government would stimulate the economy of the country by regulating business. The letters displayed above show that both Smith and Fields were aligned with the initial introduction of the NRA.

Fields maintained contact with political leaders from around the country that he was associated with at the various Democratic conventions. One letter he received was from Albert Ritchie, governor of Maryland.

ALBERT C. RITCHIE
GOVERNOR

EXECUTIVE DEPARTMENT

ANNAPOLIS, MARYLAND

September 26, 1934

Mr. Harvey G. Fields,
Chairman Public Service Commission,
Farmerville, Louisiana.

Dear Mr. Fields:

    Many thanks for your letter of September
22nd, and for your good wishes and interest
in my coming Campaign for re-election. It
was nice to hear from you again, and I recall
with much pleasure our meeting in 1928.

    With kind regards, I am,

                    Sincerely yours,

                        Albert C. Ritchie
                    Governor.

Another individual Fields was associated with who had been on the 1928 ballot was Theodore Bilbo, governor of Mississippi for two terms, and who in 1934 was running for the U.S. Senate. Bilbo was also one of the many candidates listed as a nominee for president at the 1928 convention. The letter below is from Fields congratulating Bilbo on his campaign and noting that he, Bilbo, is a friend of the farmer. At the time of the writing, Fields was also president of the Ouachita Valley Farm Relief Agency, and he was very active and concerned with the plight of the farmers. Bilbo immediately responded to Fields's letter and asked for any support Fields could provide. Bilbo was elected, and in 1935 was sent to the U.S. Senate from Mississippi. Interesting to note that Fields also referenced Bilbo's being considerate of the rights of other classes.

LOUISIANA PUBLIC SERVICE COMMISSION

HARVEY G. FIELDS, CHAIRMAN
  FARMERVILLE, LA.
WADE O. MARTIN,
  ST. MARTINVILLE, LA.
FRANCIS WILLIAMS,
  NEW ORLEANS, LA.

BATON ROUGE

P. A. FRYE, SECRETARY
  BATON ROUGE, LA.
ALEX GROUCHY,
  ASST. SECTY. AND GEN. FIELD AGENT

IN REPLY PLEASE REFER
TO OUR FILE NO.

Farmerville, Louisiana.
August 30th, 1934.

Hon. Theodore G. Bilbo,
Jackson, Miss.

Dear Sir:-

      I take this means of extending my con-
gratulations upon the splendid showing made by you
in the primary election yesterday.

      Many of your Louisiana friends and admirers,
like myself, hope you will win in the second primary,
because we believe you are sincere, a friend of the
farmer and laborer, yet considerate of the rights of
other classes, and that your election, because of
your independence and your farsightedness and your
loyalty to the democratic party would be of immense
benefit to the people of your State and to the entire
south.

      With kindest regards and wishing you success,
I am,

      Yours respectfully,

      Harvey G.Fields, Chairman, La.
      Public Service Commission.

HGF/m.

J. G. BURKETT, CAMPAIGN MANAGER
LULA WIMBERLY, SECRETARY
WILL JACOBS, TREASURER
JOHN L. SMITH, PUBLICITY DIRECTOR

Campaign Headquarters
OF
THEO. G. BILBO
CANDIDATE FOR U. S. SENATE

EXECUTIVE COMMITTEE
B. M. FULTON.
O. W. BALDWIN.
DR. H. F. GABRISON
PHIL ARMITAGE
WM. M. SNYDER

JACKSON, MISSISSIPPI

September 1, 1934.

Mr. Harvey G. Fields, Chairman,
La. Public Service Commission,
Farmerville, La.

Dear Mr. Fields:

I appreciate very deeply your message of congratulations.
The interest you have manifested in my campaign increases
my desire to dedicate my life in service to the people
of my state and nation as a member of the United States
Senate.

There is a broad field for service in that body and I
believe that I can make the people of Mississippi an acceptable servant as their United States Senator, and I
know that I will leave nothing undone that lies within my
power to bring about that result.

If you have friends in Mississippi whom you think you
may influence by a letter, I shall be very appreciative
of such letters.

Again expressing my grateful appreciation for your congratulations and for your interest in my behalf, I am

Faithfully yours,

Theo G. Bilbo

TGB:R

Fields was now actively involved in law, politics, and public service. He was chairman of the Public Service Commission, actively practicing law in Farmerville and was either a chairman of or member of various organizations that promoted the plight of farmers and laborers during dire economic conditions. His energy and drive for success was enormous. Success in any one of the endeavors would normally require total dedication. Fields was successful in all three.

Prior to the 1928 convention, Fields was known to the Democratic Party as a leader that was not only dedicated to the party but was also loyal to his own beliefs of fairness. Following the convention, his full potential was realized. This convention served as a springboard that lead to Fields's involvement in the national political arena for years to come.

CHAPTER 4

A PUBLIC SERVANT

Huey Long was extremely shrewd, understood the people he wanted to help, and realized the power of the press. He also understood that he had been elected by an electorate that was desperately needing hope for a better future. When he first took office, he was determined to change the course of the state and deliver on his campaign promises.

He inherited a poorly organized government. Large corporations would prepare legal bills and bribe politicians to introduce and pass the legislation. Many times the politicians were rewarded with jobs and money. This was a cancer that Long would take his scalpel to. He consolidated his power by firing hundreds of state employees that were identified as opponents. These firings came from heads of state agencies down through the ranks to state highway workers. Replacements consisted of his loyal followers. This helped solidify his power base at the grassroots level.

Each appointment had a cost. Every employee that was appointed owed his position on the state payroll to Long was expected to "donate" a portion of his salary to the Long political fund. These funds were placed in the famous "deduct box" that would ultimately be overseen by Seymour Weiss. Long used these funds for political purposes. Even though viewed as unethical, the purpose was totally for political advancement and was not used for personal wealth gain.

Long moved quickly to act on his campaign promises. He proved that his promises were not empty rhetoric aimed at the illiterate rural masses of Louisiana. Free textbooks for all children was first proposed by Claiborne Parish School superintendent John Patton. Long embraced the idea, and based on his own inability to enter LSU due to book costs, he pushed this legislation through the 1928 state legislature. The legality was contested, and Long took the fight to the Louisiana Supreme Court and won the appeal. This legislation was controversial in Caddo Parish, and the parish refused the charity from the state. Long responded by withholding authorization of the building of a new Army Air Corps base. The textbooks were finally accepted, and the base was ultimately built and named Barksdale. This base is still a major financial benefit for the Shreveport area and was a launching point for B52 bombers in the early days of the Gulf War in 1991.

The initial book order could not be funded. Long was not deterred, and he solicited a loan to purchase the books. He wanted to move fast, and bureaucratic red tape wouldn't stop him.

Huey also supported night classes for illiterate Louisiana and made good on a commitment to provide cheap North Louisiana gas to New Orleans. The Public Service Commission would provide support for this initiative.

He began a major highway-and-building program for the state. Bridges across the Mississippi would link a state that was split by a river that was a mile wide at many locations.

His love of LSU led to a major construction initiative. Leon Weiss, a prominent architect from Farmerville, Louisiana, was responsible for a large number of plans for the expansion of the university. Huey's resourcefulness was never more apparent than when he turned his attention to his beloved university. Federal funds could not be obtained for the construction of a new football stadium. Federal funds were available for student housing. Huey requested and received funding for the construction of student housing at LSU. It was unknown at the time that the student dorm would be built inside the new LSU football stadium. Huey got his stadium, and LSU got its dorm. The stadium is in use today. Students were housed inside the stadium through the 1950s.

There was also another story that the Ringling Brothers, Barnum and Bailey Circus, had arrived in Baton Rouge and would have its opening on the day of an LSU home football game. Huey didn't like this as it would potentially take fans away from the game. He sent a representative to ask that they delay their opening by a day. The circus protested and denied the request, noting that they couldn't afford a one-day delay. Long quickly dispatched a member of the department of agriculture to inform the circus of a state law. The law stated that any animal coming from another state must be dipped in a tick poison to prevent diseases being passed by ticks. The "dip law" did not exclude the elephants, giraffes, and large cats of a circus. The Long administrator wanted to know when the animals would be dipped, and they could not move within the state until the action had taken place. The administrator returned to the governor and notified him that he had issued an exception to the circus. The circus decided it would be best if they rested a day before opening in Baton Rouge, and the LSU football team played in front of all its fans. Long is also reported to have co-composed a song for the LSU band. The title of the song is, "Every Man a King."

By the end of 1928, Long was looking like a hero to rural Louisiana. He was determined that his programs and legislation was the right direction for the state to follow. He would show up on the floors of the House of Representatives or the Senate and would ram his legislation through the two chambers. He was relentless and tireless. It was noted that when Long practiced law, he would stay up into the early hours of the morning to ensure his case was adequately prepared. The same was noted of Fields.

Long also took on a very controversial topic. He felt that the African American should receive both educational and standard-of-living improvements. Field noted that Long had cooperated with black leaders of the state to include Dr. Clark of Southern University and Dr. C.P. Adams of Grambling. Fields further noted that Huey believed that the African Americans were entitled to a good education, property rights and proper justice in the courts. Contrary to these beliefs, Huey didn't believe that the black man should be entitled to vote. It would be Huey's brother, Earl, who twenty years later would fight on the floor of the Louisiana Legislature for the rights of the African American to get the right to vote.

Long's desire to influence his power and advance his agenda didn't stop at the state line. In 1932, Hattie Caraway had filled her dead husband's Senate seat. She had proven to be a pathfinder for women in the way that she conducted her business in Washington. She had been the first woman to preside over the Senate and used this to announce her intention to run for election to the post she had been appointed to fill. Following his commitment that he needed to help disparaged women, Huey Long said he felt sorry for the widowed lady. Opponents had attacked her and stated that she wasn't supposed to run for this office when her husband's term had ended. Huey went north to Arkansas and relentlessly campaigned for her throughout the state. She won and spent twelve years representing Arkansas in the United States Senate.

In 1928, Fields became a member of the Public Service Commission to fill the unexpired seat of Huey Long. This was a good fit for a man who felt a keen desire to raise the standards of the laboring class of an oppressed state while striving to affect the political landscape of an emerging nation. Then in 1929, Fields's energy and perseverance would be called on to expand his belief that everyone deserved the right to a decent lifestyle. It's been observed that great leaders are not recognized as great leaders unless they are in a position to lead during some great crisis. In 1929, this opportunity presented itself.

In October of 1929, one year after Harvey Fields was appointed as a member of the Public Service Commission, Wall Street crashed, and the Great Depression began. This began a ten-year period of high unemployment, poverty, deflation, lost economic growth, and an issue that especially appealed to Fields in rural Louisiana—plunging farm income and numerous foreclosures. It was also a low point in the morale and feeling of self-worth for the American farmer and laborer.

The Depression began in the United States but quickly spread throughout the world. Causes for this catastrophe are credited to high consumer debt, reduction in foreign trade, wealth inequality, lack of banking regulation, and the United States protectionist practices. The inequality of wealth had been a major battle for Huey Long. The Depression would be a springboard for his causes for justice and would expand the footprint from the labor force of Louisiana to the general populace of America.

The year 1929 was a year of challenge for Huey Long. It would also provide even more solidity for the Long political machine. Long had a vision of social programs for his state that would lift the unfortunate and lower classes of both rural and urban

Louisiana to a higher standard of living. The only problem was that social programs need funding, and Long knew one source that was untapped.

Long believed that Standard Oil had been taking advantage of the state and its residents. It would be time for Standard Oil to begin supporting the state that was supplying a major part of the company's income. In 1929, Long called a special session of the Louisiana legislature. Purpose of the session was to levy a five-cent-a-barrel tax on the oil produced in Louisiana. The state's oil interests vehemently protested and Legislator Cecil Morgan from oil-rich Shreveport moved to impeach Long. On what was named Bloody Monday, a brawl broke out in the legislature. Long had decided it might be best to adjourn and end the conflict. The legislature overruled this and voted to stay in session and proceeded with the impeachment of Huey Long.

Long took this opportunity to carry his impeachment to the court of public opinion. He went on a speaking tour and passed out circulars, stating that his impeachment was a political move by big business to stop his move for social reform.

The House of Representatives did pass several of the charges and sent the charges to the Senate. Long's ability to foresee what could potentially happen in any situation served him well. Huey was ready for the possibility of the House's vote going against him. When the charges hit the Senate, he presented a document referred to as the Round Robin. This document was signed by more than one-third of the Senate and stated that they would not vote against Long no matter what the House presented. With a two-thirds majority of the Senate required to impeach, the proceedings were over with no conviction.

It was now Long's turn. Huey rewarded the Round Robin signers with favors such as state jobs, and some allegedly received cash for their signatures of loyalty. Long then turned his attention to dealing with those that opposed him. He fired relatives of his opposition from state jobs and supported candidates to run against the opposition. The majority of the Louisiana newspapers received financial support from big business that opposed Long. Long countered this in the spring of 1930 when he launched his own paper, the *Louisiana Progress*.

Long began receiving death threats following the impeachment trial, so he started having bodyguards accompany him.

Fields was having his share of trouble in the Public Service Commission. He was running into difficulty getting his progressive efforts pushed forward. It is curious why Huey had not taken a more active stance in the early years to a commission that could provide such a vital service for the state. This would later change.

In 1930, Long proposed a major road-building effort. He had used an approach to paving small sections of roads around the state. He would then connect the paved sections with other sections and thus provide a major network of paved roads. He also understood that if rural Louisiana had an opportunity to drive on sections of paved roads, they would view Long as both a man of his word and a success in supplying a much-improved path to travel on. This would continue to grow his power base.

The bond issue presented to the 1930 legislature for capital construction was defeated. This bond issue was intended for road construction and the construction of a new state capital. The design of the capital was awarded to Leon Weiss of Farmerville, a supporter of Long during the impeachment hearing.

Long was undaunted and again took his defeat to the public to determine if his programs were important to their well-being and if his popularity was waning. In a bold move, Huey Long announced that he would run for the U.S. Senate. He told the voters that this would be a referendum to confirm his social programs. If he was defeated for the Senate race, he would also resign his position as governor. The ploy worked, and Long won the election by a margin of 57 percent to candidate and sitting senator Joseph Randell's 43 percent. Then Long announced that he would not resign his post as governor. He did not want to turn over control to Lieutenant Governor Paul Cyr, and thus he remained governor and left the Senate seat vacant. "When Randell was in office the seat was vacant anyway," Long quipped.

Huey Long was not the only individual to run for public office in 1930. Fields had been appointed to fill Long's unexpired term when Long was elected governor in 1928. This term ended in 1930, and Fields was successfully elected by popular vote to one of the three positions of Public Service Commissioner for a six-year term.

The economic outlook for rural Louisiana was looking worse by 1930. The agricultural base of rural Louisiana, coupled with the massive timber industry, was being negatively impacted by the Smoot-Hawley Tariff Act. This act was intended as a protectionist policy but caused other nations to stop purchasing American agriculture and timber products. Fields would eventually take an active role in representing the labor forces of Louisiana and opposing major policies originated in Washington. Long's vote of support, provided by the electorate in the 1930 election, renewed his determination to push his social and infrastructure programs forward. He entered into an agreement with his longtime rival, the Old Regulars. This was the same organization that had mistakenly underestimated his abilities when he first took office. Now Long was in a position of power when negotiating with the political bosses. This would continue to place him in a position of ultimate power in the state. The Old Regulars agreed to support his legislation and support his future candidates. Such enormous support didn't come without a cost. Long agreed to provide support for a bridge over the Mississippi at New Orleans, an airport for New Orleans, and money for infrastructure.

Long was moving faster to expand LSU. The enrollment grew form 1,600 to 4,000. The LSU medical school in New Orleans was founded and work scholarships were instituted, which allowed children of the poor to go to college if they desired.

By 1931, Lieutenant Governor Cyr had had enough. Cyr felt that Long needed to move on to Washington, and he needed to be named governor. Cyr, by then a devout enemy of Huey Long, declared that he was the legitimate governor of the state of Louisiana. This was a tactical blunder for Cyr but added to the mystique of Louisiana politics. Long mobilized units of the Louisiana National Guard and surrounded the capital. This physically stopped the attempt to take over power. This was reminiscent of third-world-country coup attempts but was unprecedented in American state government. Long then took his fight to the Louisiana Supreme Court. He argued that Cyr was no longer the lieutenant governor of Louisiana. When he, Cyr, had proclaimed to be the governor of Louisiana, he had effectively resigned as the lieutenant governor. The Supreme Court sided with Long, and Cyr was no longer lieutenant governor either. The lieutenant governor's position was filled with Long's friend, Louisiana senate president, Alvin Olin King.

Fields was staying very busy. He was not only a member of the Public Service Commission, he was also head of the Louisiana Fifth District Democratic Central committee, plus he was running his successful law practice in Farmerville. The law firm of Long, Fields, and O'Neal was no longer in existence.

Huey felt that his success in Arkansas with Hattie Caraway could translate to a success in Louisiana. Bolivar Kemp was a Member of the Unitied States House of Representatives. On June 19, 1933, Kemp suddenly died of a heart attach. Long, through O.K. Allen, had Kemps widow, Ester, proclaimed a winner. Allen had announced that an election would be held eight days following his announcement and then boldly named Mrs. Kemp the winner as an unapposed candidate. Allen stated that eight days would not be enough time to hold the democratic primary. The Louisiana 6th district erupted screams to lynch both Long and Allen. A revolt election was held and this was won by Jared Sanders. Both went to Washington to be seated and both were sent back to Louisiana. A U.S. House Election Committee disallowed both elections. Louisiana Representative Riley Wilson sat on the committee. Long was dismayed and disturbed to learn that Mrs. Kemp returned to her home in Amite and withdrew her name from consideration for her husband's job.

Fields had later been asked to discuss a political matter with Riley Wilson. He refused and noted that Wilson provided little or no support to the returning military and the farmers and laborers of his congressional district. Fields also wrote about the Kemp/Sanders controversy. He addressed his disdain for Wilson for the way he treated Mrs. Kemp when she went to Washington. Being the gentlemen he was, this was considered deplorable by Fieldes. Fields also noted that neither Mrs. Kemp nor Jared Sanders should have been seated when they went to Washington.

This demonstrates the independence that Fields saw in himself. He had formally stated that the candidate that Huey Long had supported and wanted to be seated should not have been seated. Harvey knew this was not a fair election and did not meet with his moral stand on election law. Few men had politically survived a contradiction to a Long proposal or questioning a Long decision. Harvey was a different individual. Not only did he survive he continued to be respected by and worked closely with Huey.

A copy of the letter follows:

LOUISIANA PUBLIC SERVICE COMMISSION

HARVEY G. FIELDS, CHAIRMAN
FARMERVILLE, LA.

WADE O. MARTIN,
ST. MARTINVILLE, LA.

FRANCIS WILLIAMS,
NEW ORLEANS, LA.

BATON ROUGE

P. A. FRYE, SECRETARY
BATON ROUGE, LA.

ALEX GROUCHY,
ASST. SECTY. AND GEN. FIELD AGENT

IN REPLY PLEASE REFER
TO OUR FILE NO.

Farmerville, Louisiana.
June 26th, 1934.

Mr. J.M.Kavanaugh,
Clay, Louisiana.

Dear Sir and Friend:-

Your letter received and beg to say
I will write Mr. Farley and Senator Overton in behalf of
Mr. Stanley, because you are asking it, as I do not know
Mr. Stanley very well.

I cannot write Mr. Wilson, for the
reason that I am against Mr. Wilson, and never ask a man
for favors when I am fighting him. I never play with a
man I am fighting in any way, so it will be impossible for
me to write Mr. Wilson, as I am very much opposed to him
and believe he should be defeated.

He forgot the War boys, the farmers
and the laborers in seventy-five percent of his votes, in
my opinion, and then stabbed the widow of his dead friend
when her name went before his Committee.

I do not think either Sanders or
Mrs. Kemp should have been seated, but Riley Wilson could
have folded his hands and in a manly way got out of it
all by stating he would not stab in the back the widow
of his old dead friend, Bolivar Kemp, but instead of that
he gloats and smiles in opposing her because he thought
it would satisfy the gang and would have seated Sanders if
he could have done so. Congress sent them both back, which
was in accordance with the law and disregarded Mr. Wilson's
intentions to kick the woman out by herself. So for these
reasons I cannot take it up with him however much I would
like to do anything I could for you. I believe it is honest
to fight him and ask for no favors.

With kindest regards,

HGF/m

Your friend,

Harvey G.Fields.

By 1932, the flurry of activity in Fields's life had reached a frenzy pitch. He was working in several endeavors that any one would have consumed an average person, plus he was providing support for the Long organization.

James A. Noe was a good friend of Fields's. Noe's wife taught at Farmerville prior to meeting Noe and had taught Fields's young son. When Noe first moved to Louisiana in 1922, he lived in Farmerville for several years. Noe was little known to Long in 1932. What Noe represented to Long was that he was a candidate for public office that was competing against two staunch Long adversaries.

Mathew Redmond was an able lawyer who was a pronounced adversary of Long. Like Redmond, Wood Thompson was also an adversary of Long's and was likewise an excellent lawyer. Noe was no lawyer but was a very savvy and successful businessman. Redmond and Thompson would be competing for the same position as Noe.

Prior to the 1932 election, Noe had moved to Monroe and was running for the senate seat in Ouachita and Jackson parishes. This included the Louisiana towns of Monroe and Jonesboro. Long drove to Farmerville to meet with Fields. Noe was having a hard time with his bid for the senate seat, and Long wanted Fields to help Noe with the campaign. His adversaries had launched a vicious attack on Noe, and Noe needed a strong ally. Fields agreed and went on the campaign trail for Noe. He set up campaign rallies, gave speeches, and spoke on the radio. When the election was finally held, Noe won by a majority over both candidates. Noe became very close to Huey and was a Long insider at the time of Long's death. Noe and Long had also formed a business partnership linked to the oil and gas industry.

Although Long had fought the large oil companies that he felt were taking advantage of the state, Noe's initial major financial success came from his investment in the large Monroe gas field. The field was then the largest gas field in Louisiana, and Noe became wealthy in an industry that was relentlessly attacked by Long. Noe was not single-minded, and his business successes proved this to be true. James "Jimmy" A. Noe later founded KNOE Television and Radio in Monroe. He was a pathfinder in the industry, and his television station in Monroe was the first in North Central Louisiana and South Central Arkansas. He also founded WNOE television in New Orleans. Additionally, Noe was a successful rancher in North Louisiana.

Fields's activities in 1932 didn't stop with his law practice, Democratic Party activities, Public Service Commission job, and providing support for the Louisiana 1932 campaign. Fields had to prepare for the 1932 Democratic National Convention.

The 1932 convention was similar to the 1928 Convention for the Louisiana delegation. Huey Long was there, as was Fields. Once again, the Long organization had its set of delegates, and another organization sent their set of delegates. In 1928, Robert Ewing stood with Fields as delegation leaders. In 1932, Ewing's son, John D., led the opposition delegation. Louisiana was not the only delegation with controversy. Minnesota, likewise, had a controversial delegation.

Carter Glass, senator from Virginia, once again attacked the Long delegation just as he had done in the 1928 delegation. Fields noted that the state delegations from Alabama, Georgia, Kansas, Kentucky, Michigan, Pennsylvania, and Wisconsin were instrumental in seating the Long Louisiana delegation. Fields also noted that his friend James Farley performed the important and almost-impossible task of pulling the leadership of the two Louisiana Democratic delegations together into a cohesive force.

The seating of the Long delegation was important to Franklin Delano Roosevelt. Roosevelt had dropped support for Al Smith and decided to run himself. Smith was still on the ballot and was a thorn in the side for Roosevelt and felt that Roosevelt had let him down. After three votes, Roosevelt still did not have enough delegates to become the candidate. Roosevelt had significant support from Senators Wheeler, Hull, Barkley, and Long. Long not only had the influence of his state but also the influence of other states in the Deep South.

A candidate that was receiving quite a lot of attention was John Nance Garner, Speaker of the U.S. House of Representatives. William McAdoo from California and legendary publishing magnate William Randolph Hurst were both supporting Garner.

After several days of debates and deliberation, Joseph P. Kennedy contacted Hurst. He explained that if the convention continued as it did, there was a distinct possibility that Smith or Cleveland mayor Newton Baker could be the party's nominee. Hurst contacted Garner and convinced him to bow out of the race. When McAdoo heard of Garner's decision, he immediately had the California delegation support Roosevelt. Other delegations fell in line with Roosevelt, and on the fourth vote, Franklin Delano Roosevelt became the Democratic Party's candidate for president.

Fields jumped on the bandwagon for Roosevelt and worked diligently to elect a Democratic president. This was a success, and soon after Roosevelt was elected president on a vote of hope for the country, Fields received a letter from the president-elect. This mimeographed letter follows.

Roosevelt presented himself as the person that could deliver America from the throes of the Great Depression. His speeches gave hope to America in their greatest time of need just as Huey Long had been doing to the residents of Louisiana for years. Fields knew that these two dynamic individuals would provide the leadership to lift the lives of the downtrodden and the oppressed. This marriage would be short-lived.

Louisiana also had a new governor in 1932. Oscar Kelly "O. K." Allen was elected governor of the state. Allen had been handpicked by Long to assume the leadership of Louisiana.

By the time this letter reaches you, the critical moment of this presidential election will have arrived and from now on the responsibility of our success lies almost entirely, not with the leaders of our Party, not even with the leaders of our state organizations, but in the hands of our local committeemen and women and on their shoulders rests the responsibility of getting the voters to the polls.

Not all of the great meetings that have been held throughout the country, not all the radio speeches which have reached the ears of tens of millions of our voters, not all the pamphlets arguing our case that have been broadcast throughout the country will be effective in securing the triumph of the Democratic Party without your active cooperation in seeing that the votes which these very efforts have brought over to our side, are actually placed in the ballot box on election day.

By all the signs, by all the tests which are used to forecast election results, we are on the eve of a great triumph for our Party. But at this final moment the one thing which brings to me confidence and assurance of success, is the feeling that our local committeemen and women who are the actual representatives, not only of the democracy of the state but of the nation as well, have entered into this fight with zeal, with intelligence and with determination to see that all that has been done is not wasted by indifference and apathy on election day. In you I place my confidence and my trust.

From the reports of your state leaders, from the many letters which I have received from those who took my invitation to write me in the sincere spirit in which it was meant, I feel confident that never before has the Party come to the polls with such an earnest, militant fighting body of local committeemen and women as we have this year. I feel sure that you have done your best and are going to do your best and no matter what the result may be, it is my purpose to write you individually and thank you for your unselfish services.

I am asking your County Chairman to report to your State Chairman the names of those who have been particularly diligent in the cause as shown by the increase in the Democratic vote in their districts as compared with previous years and I have asked the State Chairmen in turn to forward such

names to me that I may in addition to my letter of thanks, express a feeling of obligation and gratitude which all your leaders have towards you as some slight reward for particularly noteworthy service. I feel sure that your name will be on that list.

If there is any last thing which you feel we should do in your particular territory, please write me, or if you feel it is very urgent, telegraph using the same address as before, 49 East 65th St., New York City.

There is every reason to believe that the people of this country are determined to replace the baffled and inefficient efforts of the present administration with those who believe in the capacity of the people to bring an end to the long period of depression by united effort and who will replace promises with deeds.

All during election day my thoughts will be very much with you who are on the field of battle bringing up our forces to the ballot boxes, and if victory is ours, my first feeling of thankfulness will be for the efforts which you have made in this campaign.

Yours very sincerely,

Franklin D. Roosevelt

Fields's life took another turn in 1932. As if he wasn't already engaged in a myriad of activities, he would soon be working tirelessly to bring relief to the multitude of Americans that were looking for relief in the depths of the Great Depression. In 1932, Fields would be named as the chairman of the Public Service Commission.

The following press release appeared in Louisiana newspapers.

FIELDS SLATED FOR CHAIRMAN

Harvey G. Fields of Farmerville, member of the state public service commission from the North Louisiana district, is slated as the chairman of the new commission immediately after it organizes following the general election in November.

It is also rumored that all the commissioners' employees will be swept out of office except Mrs. Hazel N. Albritton, secretary for the North Louisiana district of which Mr. Fields is commissioner.

The report of these developments followed a conference of several hours late Wednesday of last week in the office of Governor O. K. Allen, between the governor, Senator Huey P. Long, Mr. Fields and Wade O. Martin, recently nominated to the commission from the second district Dudley. LeBlanc, incumbent. It is also reported that Mr. Martin will be named vice chairman.

Mr. Fields, while reticent to discuss the conference, did state when asked about the matter that "it is probable that the chief executive of the state will order a complete audit of the workings of the state public service commission, and the financial disbursements of the commission for the last 12 months, and if such is the case I heartily welcome the audit, and will take great pleasure in assisting in any audit of investigation made."

"I took no part in the issuance of $20,000 to $25,000 worth of certificates now the subject of controversy. I voted against the resolution authorizing their issuance, and gave the legal opinion that they were without any force and effect and also invalid."

Besides the rumors of the new appointees and the contemplated probe, it was also reported that it is probable that Senator Long and Governor Allen will have the public service, which has jurisdiction over navigation projects and rates, so enlarge the commission's duties as to assist in flood relief works, and that Mr. Fields would take part in that class of work at Washington, in concert with Senator Long and Senator Overton, and that Senator Long would assist the commission in matters before the interstate commerce commission.

It is reported that at present there is an act pending before congress and passed by the lower house, placing the regulation of buses and truck lines largely before the interstate commerce commission, which act provides, in cases affecting various states, that a commissioner from each state will sit with the interstate commerce commission, as a special judge and commissioner. In the event this becomes a law Mr. Fields, it was indicated, will as chairman of the Louisiana commission, be designated to represent Louisiana in all cases of this kind.

Further than the statement mentioned above, Mr. Fields declined to discuss the conference held in the governor's office, except to say that is was "harmonious" and that "the new commission will seek to dispose of the 240 cases now on the commission docket."

Following his appointment as chairman, a niece sent a letter of congratulations to Fields. True to the family spirit, the niece was in government service of the United States Treasury Department and was identified as a supervisor of permits for the Bureau of Industrial Alcohol.

TREASURY DEPARTMENT

BUREAU OF INDUSTRIAL ALCOHOL

OFFICE OF
SUPERVISOR OF PERMITS
DISTRICT No

IN REPLY REFER TO

New Orleans, La.,
12/1/32.

Dear Uncle Harvey:

Just to let you "in" on our business affairs, I am enclosing a copy of a letter which is self-explanatory. You probably won't be interested - in which event, tear the letter up and forget it.

I was glad to know that you were made Chairman of the Public Service Commission - think you deserved it.

Remember me very kindly to your family.

Best wishes,

Fields would still fight for the rights of the individual with his law practice. Soon after being selected as the chairman of the Public Service Commission, he received an opportunity to plead to the Louisiana Supreme Court the conviction of Monroe White in a North Louisiana murder case.

No. 32,425

Supreme Court of Louisiana

STATE OF LOUISIANA,

Appellee,

versus

MONROE WHITE,

Defendant and Appellant.

Appeal from Third Judicial District Court, Union Parish, Louisiana; Hon. E. L. Walker, Judge.

ORIGINAL BRIEF ON BEHALF OF DEFENDANT, MONROE WHITE.

HARVEY G. FIELDS,
Farmerville, Louisiana;
ELDER & ELDER,
Ruston, Louisiana;
SCARBAROUGH & BARHAM,
Ruston, Louisiana;
Attorneys for Defendant-Appellant.

HAUSER PRINTING CO., NEW ORLEANS

CHAPTER 5

THE ACTIVE YEARS
A CHAIRMAN, THE FEDERAL GOVERNMENT,
AND A BULLET

In 1932, Louisiana was in the middle of a statewide election. Huey wanted to ensure that he was leaving the state in the hands of someone that would continue his programs and who would also immediately respond to his edicts. Long selected childhood friend Oscar Kelly "O. K." Allen. If he was able to get Allen elected, he would assign a loyal and ambitious New Orleans lawyer to become Allen's secretary. Long's selection for that position was Richard Leche. Allen would then be in office, and Leche would be supporting Allen. Leche would also be reporting to Long as to what was happening in the administration. Long would be assured of maintaining his power over the state.

Long went to his war chest and provided financial support for Allen. He also used his communication channels to give the grassroots support that would be required to deliver a governorship to Allen. Fields received a personal letter from Long requesting help for Allen and giving directions as to what he expected to be done. The letterhead identified that the OK Allen campaign headquarters were located at the Roosevelt Hotel in New Orleans. This hotel was managed by Seymour Weiss, a Long insider and later treasurer of several of Long's private political funds.

CAMPAIGN HEADQUARTERS OF

O. K. ALLEN
CANDIDATE FOR GOVERNOR

1262 Roosevelt Hotel
New Orleans, La.   January 6, 1932.

P e r s o n a l .

Mr. H. G. Fields,
Farmerville, La.

Dear Friend,

ALLEN J. ELLENDER
HARVEY PELTIER
STATE CAMPAIGN MANAGERS

RICHARD W. LECHE
CITY CAMPAIGN MANAGER

Complete the Work Ticket

For
GOVERNOR
O. K. ALLEN

For
LIEUTENANT GOVERNOR
JOHN B. FOURNET

For
ATTORNEY GENERAL
G. L. PORTERIE

For
REGISTRAR OF LAND OFFICE
LUCILLE MAE GRACE

For
TREASURER
JESS S. CAVE

For
STATE AUDITOR
L. B. BAYNARD, JR.

For
SUPERINTENDENT PUBLIC EDUCATION
T. H. HARRIS

For
COMMISSIONER OF AGRICULTURE
HARRY D. WILSON

For
SECRETARY OF STATE
E. A. CONWAY

         I am sending you a package of election literature and buttons that I want you to have well scattered throughout your Parish during these closing days of the election. This package contains all the old literature and some new that we have, but I want you to have it neatly and properly handed around all over the Parish. If you have to hire some one, then if our friends haven't any money, I will pay for it, for I want this to be done. Let the literature get out. It puts the facts before the people to off-set eleventh hour lies.

         Now, I am sending to you a separate package containing our Complete the Work Tickets to be used on election day. I am enclosing one of them. These are being sent out in envelopes throughout the Parish and you should try to see that your ballots reach the people when they vote.

         Now, old friend, don't fail me now on getting this literature scattered out to everybody. Do this as quickly as you can because I am going to send out the Louisiana Progress very soon.

         Now, this Louisiana Progress will reach you middle of next week. Arrange now, while you are arranging to distribute the literature, to have these newspapers handed out properly. You will be sent 1,000 copies of the Progress. They should reach the people as quickly as you get them. Also, if need be, I will pay for them to be handed out, if you cannot do so other-wise, but please get them out.

         This stuff costs all the money we have, and some more. Don't let it waste, please. Get it out to the people.

         Your friend,

Huey P. Long.

Interesting to note that Long noted that this election was using all the money that was in his political funds. Long would reference political finances on several occasions and display his understanding of the cost of politics. It also highlights that Long didn't use the deep pockets of big business to fund his political activities. Had he done so, the financial concerns would not have been such an important topic in his correspondence. Fields had also received a note from Long addressing reports that Long was extremely wealthy and using government money to circulate his speeches and literature. Long denied both allegations and explains this in the note.

HUEY P. LONG
UNITED STATES SENATOR
WASHINGTON, D. C.

Dear Friend:

Two reports are repeatedly published in the newspapers and announced in programs rendered by the big
interests in their radio programs. The first report is
that I am a man of great means. If I could sell everything I own (which is not much), I could not pay one
half of my debts.

The other report repeatedly printed and circulated is that the speeches and literature which I send
out are printed at government expense. That statement
is also false. With the exception of government
bulletins, etc., everything we send out, including the
enclosed document, must be paid for by us. We are
frequently unable to pay some of our printing accounts
and therefore have to delay sending out articles requested of us until we can find money with which to do
so. That fact can be verified by the accounts we
have owed to the Government Printing Office.

We do not make any solicitation of you for any
help and are glad of the privilege to send anything
we can on request absolutely free, in the hope that
those who feel that our cause is just will make known
to their neighbors some of the facts which we furnish.

Yours sincerely,

U. S. Senator.

(Reprint from Congressional Record Jan. 14, 1935)

Fields, as did others from across the state, did what was required to support the Allen ticket. The final outcome was a win for Allen and a win for Long. Soon after taking office, Allen met with Long and Fields. The frustrations that Fields had over the inability of the Public Service Commission to have the drive and foresight to promote his social reforms were now over. Everyone on the Public Service Commission except Fields and his district secretary were swept from their positions. Fields was made chairman of the commission and at the same time presented with expanded commission duties.

In 1932, the Great Depression was at the very lowest point. Human self-worth was being challenged on every street corner and farm in the nation. Despair was rampant, and the country was desperately looking for leaders that could lead it out of these horrible conditions. In 1932, Franklin Delano Roosevelt was elected to become the President of the United States, Huey Long took office as the United States senator; O. K. Allen became governor of Louisiana, and Harvey G. Fields became chairman of the Louisiana Public Service Commission and chairman of the Fifth District Democratic State Committee. Although Fields had displayed extreme intestinal fortitude and immense devotion to duty, his real work was just beginning.

Huey Long arrived in Washington in January of 1932, and the firestorm began. His same passion that surrounded his early days of taking on the power brokers in Louisiana was now refocused to taking on the wealthy elite. During the 1932 elections, Long had aligned with Roosevelt and gave full support for his election. Fields likewise set up Roosevelt support groups and actively politicked for Roosevelt and his doctrine. When the polls closed in Louisiana, Roosevelt had more than 90 percent of the votes cast between himself and Herbert Hoover. Roosevelt's inauguration speech gave hope to the nation and in March of 1933 Roosevlet proclaimed, "the only thing we have to fear is fear itself"

Long and Fields both gave great respect to the belief that politics should not be gender specific. Fields communicated with Nellie Ross, who became the first female governor of the United States and was a vice chairman of the Democratic National Committee. Long was instrumental in getting Hattie Caraway of Arkansas elected as the first female United States senator.

Following Huey's death Hattie Caraway spoke at the dedication of his statue in Statutory hall in Washington. Field noted that she stated, "Let me say, to the credit of Senator Long, that he never sought to take legislative or political advantage of his assistance to me in that election. (referring to his support getting her elected to the United States Senate) To the contrary, when it so happened that I disagreed with him he showed no displeasure, but praised me for doing that which I thought was right." This was the same professional courtesy that Huey displayed towards Fields. Long and Roosevelt's close working relationship was short-lived. Quickly, Long realized that there would be no redistribution of wealth. Instead of being a supporter of Roosevelt and his doctrines, Long became a vocal critic.

By 1933, Roosevelt considered Long to be a demagogue. Very few politicians would publicly question Roosevelt's programs. One of the few that did was Huey Long. Long felt that the Federal Reserve Bank was a major factor in the unfair distribution of wealth and was one of the causes of the Great Depression. The Glass-Steagall banking act was introduced during the 1933 Congress. Long waged an unprecedented three-week filibuster against the bill. At a later time, Fields would fight one of the authors of the bill, Carter Glass, on the floor of a Democratic convention. Fields had successfully supported Long, who defeated Glass's attempt to not seat the Long delegation in the 1928 convention. He also fought Glass's attempt to prevent Gene Tallmadge's Georgia delegation from being seated. Glass wanted to write Gene Tallmadge out of the convention. Fields again took on the influential, arrogant, and articulate Senator Glass in a debate at the convention. Glass underestimated Fields, and Tallmadge was seated.

Roosevelt's "First New Deal" began in 1933 and was aimed as a quick-hit, short-term recovery for the nation. This included banking reform laws, emergency relief, agriculture programs, and the NRA, or National Recovery Administration. Fields first promoted the NRA. He had written to Al Smith in 1933, complementing him on his support of the NRA. This support would soon change. When the chairmanship of the Public Service Commission was given to Fields, he saw this as a mandate to provide relief for the misfortunate; and in 1933, the number of misfortunates in America was immense.

The Emergency Relief Administration (ERA) oversaw the Civilian Conservation Corps in Louisiana. The CCC was a program that put many to work immediately and would provide much-needed reforestation to a country that had abused its timber resources. Fields felt that several residents of Union Parish were unable to register for the CCC and wanted an explanation of why this happened. The executive director of the ERA in Louisiana sent a very detailed explanation of the role of the CCC and assured Fields that individuals who would like to register for CCC work would be allowed to do so. Fields was not afraid to take the fight to any agency when he felt it was administering its duties in an unfair manner, or where the rights of the citizenship were not respected.

EMERGENCY RELIEF ADMINISTRATION
OF THE STATE OF LOUISIANA

1409 CANAL BANK BUILDING

NEW ORLEANS, LA.

MAIN 2145

November 24, 1933

HARRY J. EARLY
Execution Director
—————
JAMES H. CRUTCHER
Associate Director

Mr. Harvey G. Fields
Farmerville, Louisiana

Dear Mr. Fields:

Copies of the letters which have been sent to you from Mr.
Sonderegger and Mr. Parsons have been sent to this office.
Mr. Sonderegger has given you a very complete outline of the
work done by the boys in the C. C. C. camps. I might add
that all junior recruits were selected from the relief rolls.
The parish quotas were based on a percentage of population
and relief rolls. Efforts were made to select boys from
those families who were in the greatest need. Our parish
relief directors submitted names of boys whose families were
receiving relief to the recruiting officers. The final selection depended upon their ability to pass the necessary examination and to meet the qualifications established by the
Government for boys to be recruited in these camps.

If there are any young men in your parish as stated in your
letter of October 31 who were unable to register with the
C. C. C. camps, I would appreciate it if you would submit
these names to Miss Cassell and I feel sure she could give
you a satisfactory explanation in each case. If such boys
were on our relief rolls, Miss Cassell would know all the
facts concerning them. If they were not, of course she
would have no means of giving you such information.

I might add that the experienced woodsmen did not have to
be selected from the relief rolls. However, in most instances, our State Forestry and our National Park representatives cooperated with our relief office in the selection
of such men. Sometimes it was impossible to find men with
the qualifications necessary for the responsibilities which
they had to assume as experienced woodsmen, on our rolls.
In such instances these men were selected from the group of
unemployed who have not yet applied to the relief offices.

I can assure you that we would be glad to make every effort
to clear up any situation in a parish which pertains to our
office, and I hope that you will feel free to call upon us
to assist you in such instances.

Sincerely yours,

Lillie H. Mairne
Associate State Director of Relief

LHN:mw

Roosevelt tapped Hugh Johnson as the man to lead a major part of the NRA. At the time of the appointment, Johnson had proved himself a worthy candidate. He had helped design the 1917 Selective Service Act while on active duty with the United States Army. In 1919, he retired with the rank of brigadier general. Johnson entered private industry and then campaigned for Franklin Roosevelt in 1932.

The emblem of the NRA was a large eagle that was quickly recognized throughout the country. In 1933, a candidate for mayor of New York City was using the emblem in the campaign. This infuriated Fields as he saw emblems of the federal government as being public trusts and not for the use of political gains. When Johnson had the use of the emblem stopped in the New York campaign, Fields sent a letter to Johnson congratulating him.

The 1933, cover of *Time* magazine displayed General Johnson. Later that year, Fields had lost confidence in the NRA program. Johnson had been reported as using the Italian Fascist corporativism as a loose model for his programs.

By 1934, Fields was disappointed in the relief provided by the NRA to Louisiana farmers, laborers, and small-business owners. He was not witnessing the support he felt was required to provide assistance during the depths of the Great Depression. In September 1934, Fields wrote the chairman of the Textile Strike Committee, commending the stand taken against Hugh Johnson. He also stressed that Johnson needed to be replaced.

His administration was seriously failing by 1934. Contradictions in NRA policies plus rumors of heavy drinking finally led to his demise.

LOUISIANA PUBLIC SERVICE COMMISSION

HARVEY G. FIELDS, CHAIRMAN
FARMERVILLE, LA.

WADE O. MARTIN,
ST. MARTINVILLE, LA.

FRANCIS WILLIAMS,
NEW ORLEANS, LA.

BATON ROUGE

P. A. FRYE, SECRETARY
BATON ROUGE, LA.

ALEX GROUCHY,
ASST. SECTY. AND GEN. FIELD AGENT

IN REPLY PLEASE REFER
TO OUR FILE NO.

Farmerville, Louisiana.
September 20th, 1934.

Mr. Francis J. Gorman,
Chairman Textile Strike Committee,
Washington, D. C.

Dear Sir:-

You are to be complimented on your bold
and frank condemnation of some of the policies of
the NRA and thousands of citizens in the South
join you in your prayers that there will be a
change, and that some day Mr. Johnson will be
removed.

We certainly hope that some day a few
of these brain trusters will be turned out the
back door of governmental affairs, and that our
good and great leader President Roosevelt, will
then be able to carry on his plans without any
hindrances, and be able to help the people as he
so much desires to do and is trying to do.

Yours respectfully,

Harvey G. Fields, Chairman 5th
Democratic Congressional Executive
Committee of Louisiana.

HGF/hna....

Roosevelt replaced Hugh Johnson in October 1934. Fields wrote to Farley, congratulating both Farley and Roosevelt for removing him.

Farmerville, Louisiana,
October 2nd, 1934.

Honorable James A. Farley,
Chairman Democratic Committee,
Washington, D. C.

Dear Sir:-

          Congratulations to you and the President
upon the final departure of Hugh S. Johnson as head
of the NRA.

          He may have meant well, but his cause was
detrimental to business, to the Democratic Party and
to the general policies of our distinguished leader,
Mr. Roosevelt, and his military style in business
affairs was not conducive of achieving success, and
however much his employees may miss him the people are
glad he is out and does not head the department any
more.

          With kindest regards, and best wishes,
and hoping that our party may succeed in conquering
the depression, I am

                         Yours very truly,

                         Harvey G. Fields, Chairman Fifth
                         Congressional Democratic Committee
                         of Louisiana.

HGF/bhs....

Copies sent to: C. A. Stair, New Orleans, La.
                 J. N. Campbell, Shreveport, La.
                 J. E. McClanahan, Columbia, La.

Also in 1933, Fields was being nationally recognized for his work in leading the
Louisiana Public Service Commission.

September 18th, 1933.

National Magazine of Commerce
18th Twenty-first Street,
New York City, N. Y.

Gentlemen:-

                    Attention: Mr. Preston Rogers

          Your letter of the 8th concerning feature
article received, and beg to thank you for having carefully
and favorably studied my record as Chairman of the Louisiana
Public Service Commission.

          I have recently received commendation from other
magazines in Washington, and also from one of our splendid
papers in this state, so that I am indeed thankful to the
press in having given my activities their approval,
particularly at a time when public officials have so much
criticism to meet with, contentions to cope with, and
extra problems confronting them.

          I did not receive a copy of the article, and
so I am not in a position to approve or disapprove the
facts, and will appreciate you sending me copy of same at
your earliest convenience.

                    Yours respectfully,

                    Harvey G. Fields, Chairman
                    Public Service Commission.

HGF/hna...

By the end of 1933, the Roosevelt administration and Huey Long had completely broken all ties. Roosevelt stated that Long and Douglas McArthur were the two most dangerous men in America. Roosevelt later compared Huey to Adolf Hitler and Benito Mussolini. Long had infuriated Roosevelt, and Roosevelt retaliated against Long when he stopped him from participating in discussion on the distribution of federal funds and patronage for Louisiana.

Fields was distressed with the plight of the farmers and small businessmen in the rural South. Fields wanted action for these people that were in a perilous predicament. What he didn't want was bureaucratic red tape that stymied the help that was so drastically needed by the financially strapped laborer, farmer, and small businessman. He wrote a letter asking to be removed from the list of approved lawyers that would perform legal business in support of the Federal Land Bank. This was an ethical decision and displayed his integrity. The protest would certainly affect his personal finances, but Fields was the type of person that placed idealism above personal benefit. This action is reminiscent of Clarence Darrow's action when he left a lucrative job as a railroad corporate lawyer to take the case of a railroad worker against the railroad. Fields was in good company of other crusaders for rights of the labor class: Darrow and the railroads, Long and Standard Oil, and Fields and the Federal Land Bank.

Farmerville, Louisiana.
October 10th, 1933.

Federal Land Bank,
New Orleans, Louisiana.

Gentlemen:

          Inasmuch as I have understood that my name
was connected with the list of approved attorneys of
the Home Loan Bank and Federal Land Bank, and because
of the fact that I am not in accord with the delays,
red tape exercised, and the policies of the said banks,
and cannot agree with the practices and policies of
the executives of said banks, I am asking that my name
be stricken from the list of attorneys, if the same
is so listed.

          I cannot agree with the policies of your
bank in refusing loans in the Boeuf Basin District,
changes in policies made more stricter, almost precluding
help to the farmers in his worst hours of need and
distress, and for that reason I do not choose to in
anyway co-operate as long as the present policies
are pursued.

                         Yours respectfully,

                         Harvey G. Fields.

HGF/hna....

As if Fields wasn't busy enough with the assignments he had in 1932, he was named chairman of the Ouachita Valley Farm Organization. This was his lightning rod to attack the government for inefficiencies and what he considered to be the government's abuses against the working class of America. The following press release was prepared by Fields in an effort to pull the farmers in Louisiana and Mississippi together and deliver the message that Washington needed to be more supportive in the plight of these people. There was too much red tape, too much bureaucracy, and too little help; and the farmer was suffering. Fields was advocating a one-year moratorium against home, farm, and plantation foreclosures.

Not only was the United States gripped in the Great Depression but the Farmers of Louisiana and America were gripped in the worst drought in recorded history. Fields was obsessed with the fact that the Congressman from his district, Riley Wilson. Fields was adamant that Wilson was doing nothing for the plight of the farmer that was being hit by poor economic times and then having to bear the added strain of poor to no crop production.

Fields praised Pat Harrison in the address. Harrison was a staunch supporter of the labor class in Mississippi, was chairman of the Senate Finance Committee and helped carve out the Social Security System. Like Fields, Harrison supported Al Smith during the 1928 presidential campaign and actively campaigned for him throughout the South. He is also credited with swinging Mississippi to Roosevelt in the 1932 convention. Fields was present at the same convention and worked to support Roosevelt both at the convention and at the state level during the election. It was Pat Harrison that would welcome Roosevelt to Mississippi during his Southern Swing and it was at Harrison's home that Roosevelt would rendevouz with Louisiana's Richard Leche.

Fields had also supported Theodore Bilbo due to Bilbo's stance on labor. This demonstrates how Fields would align to a cause and not be attached to a specific person. In this case it was the support of the laboring class in the deep South. Bilbo and Harrison were both from Mississippi, both served in the Senate, both highly supportive of laboring America and both detested each other. The contempt was so severe that the two would not speak to each other and this ultimately led to Harrison's defeat as the U. S. Senate majority leader in 1937. Harrison lost by one vote when he refused to ask Bilbo to endorse him. He stated that he would not ask Bilbo for support even if it meant that it would cost him the Presidency for the United States.

Harvey was not shy nor would he mince words when it came to a cause that he believed to be just. Likewise, he would identify changes that he felt had to be made when a problem existed. In the following letter he" calls for the removal of the president of the Federal Land Bank.

He also called for the removal of the president of the Federal Land Bank. A copy of his address follows.

Farm Relief Committee Chairman Condemns Policies Of Federal
Land Bank. Advocates Redemption Period For Land Owners
Whose Farms Are Sold Under The Hammer.
Declares Federal Land Bank President and Managers Should Be
Removed. Appeals to Citizens To assist Government
Authorities And The President In Recovery Moves.

Harvey G. Fields, head of the Ouachita Valley Farm Relief
Committee, a recent visitor to Washington, D. C., who has taken an
active part in Louisiana in supporting all measures of benefit to
landowners, farmers, bank depositors, residents of the flood areas,
and a proponent of reductions of land taxes, reduction of governmental
expenses, local and statewide, in a statement recently issued in the
month of September says:

To The Landowners of Mississippi and Louisiana:

"Conditions in the cotton belt are in a state of chaos,
strife and financial disaster. Low prices of farm products, a rise in
cost of products and commodities bought by farmers, high taxes, and no
decrease in parish or county governmental expenses, with the cold
blooded policies of high powered Federal Land Bank executives, have
brought the farmers of the South down to a state below the standing
they justly deserve."

"They, who have been the backbone of our civilization are
now being trampled upon, their homes under mortgage, some sold, never
to be redeemed, while smiling bank officials, toss their pleas aside,
following the tossing act with words of cynicism and sarcasm."

"As chairman of a Louisiana Relief Committee I have
forwarded several times to the Federal Land Bank of New Orleans appeals
for help to the Landowners of North Louisiana, asking that some of the
million red tape rules be dispensed with, requesting that foreclosures
be suspended, that farmers in the flooded area be given a chance to
secure reasonable loans, under safe and proper conditions, but to all
of these pleas a GREAT BIG DEAF EAR was turned. My recent trip to
Washington learned me a great deal. Mr. Landowner, Mr. Farmer if you
will take your story to Washington you will win. Write your Congressman,
ask him to call on Secretary Wallace, to make an appeal that loans be
made the planters and landowners of the Boeuf Basin and Atchafalaya
Districts in Louisiana. You are entitled to them. Help me to get
removed from the management and directorate of the Federal Land Bank
men like R. B. Clarke, President of that Bank, whose policies are not
for the best interests of the Farmers of Louisiana and Mississippi."

"Seantor Pat Harrison is a friend of the Southern Planter.
If you are from Mississippi write your congressmen and your senators to
work for the removal of Clarke as head of the bank. Do not delay.
We can win if we assert ourselves. The landowners of Northeast Louisiana
and of West Mississippi are suffering as they have never suffered before,
much entitled to immediate help. President Roosevelt is their friend,
but he must be appealed to, properly informed, and the true facts
unfolded before we can hope to obtain his help."

"Stand By The President and Our Constituted Authorities in
every move made to retain an orderly system of government, to preserve
and maintain business, to check crime and wrong doing, and for a
recovery of favorable conditions of the past."

"Let each reader of this statement write Secretary Wallace
of the Department of Agriculture, Washington, D. C. appealing for land
loans, without extra red tape, almost prohibitive, to our farmers as
early as possible and before more of them lose their homes. Send him
this circular with your positive expression you are in accord with the
same, and if you get an extra copy pass it to your neighbor with the
same request."

"There is too much red tape in Federal Loan Systems. Ask
them to remove some of it. Federal Land Bank Officials like Clarke are
slapping you farmers, so to speak, in the face. Ask for the removal of
R. B. Clarke, and you will have advanced a considerable distance toward
the goal of victory."

"Ask your state representative or senator to vote for a one
year moratorium at the next session of the legislature on farm foreclosures, or else a permanent one year redemption period in which to
redeem your homes, farms and plantations after they are sold under the
hammer, and a law to protect your bank accounts and the money you get
for your cotton, potatoes and corn, you have to work so hard for, after
you have placed it on deposit in some local or great big city bank,
where the officials do not give a continental for you or anything else
except your money."

"This old stuff that the Federal Land Bank is delayed
because the farmers have not had their abstracts of title prepared is
the same old bunk that olive oil and slicked tongued bankers and
politicians use when they get in a tight corner, or find no other
reason to advance, that is they grasp at whatever they can, dump the load
back on the poor farmer and land owner, showing that in all instances
their least pity and sympathy is for the man who is at their mercy,
the high taxed and heavily mortgaged land owner. A man who owns a home
in town and his brother in the country, have the very best securities
to offer, yet they are the least considered by the FEDERAL LAND BANK
AUTHORITIES at this time and the BIG BANKER who prefers to play with
the UTILITIES and the STOCK and BOND CROWD."

"Early aid to the farmer, first aid, temporary moratoriums,
quick loans, lower valuations, better prices for farm products.
These should be our slogans."

(signed)   Harvey G. Fields.

Farmerville also had a farmer committee that was founded to help the plight of
the local farmers. Rosa Lee Forman was identified as the secretary, and her name
accompanied several documents, but no chairman was ever identified. What is known
is that Fields was actively involved with this organization. This organization had called
for several of the reforms that Fields had solicited in his capacity as chairman of the
Ouachita Valley Farm Relief Committee. A copy of a letter to Forman from Huey Long
is attached and identifies Long addressing the Fields-sponsored recommendation
that a moratorium be put in place on farm foreclosures.

United States Senate

COMMITTEE ON THE JUDICIARY

———

LOUISIANA OFFICE: 822 PERDIDO STREET

NEW ORLEANS, LA.

September 10, 1934.

Mrs. Rosa Lee Forman,
Farmerville, La.

My dear Mrs. Forman:

I have before me copy of your petition, as well as copy of Mr. Beeland's letter, which I trust is satisfactory.

I can only add that the State of Louisiana is also anxious to lend a helping hand, and has passed legislation giving everybody two years' time on their debts and preventing their property from being sold for such debts during this depression.

With best wishes, I am

Sincerely your friend,

HPL:MBW

Rosa Lee Forman was in her early twenties when the committee was formed. It is highly unlikely that due to the level of coordination required and the gender bias at that time that she would have formed this organization. Instead it was most likely that Fields had organized the group, wrote the letters requesting support and used her name as the secretary to reduce the amount of correspondence going to Washington under his name. The letter style is classical Harvey Fields. The response that Forman had received from Long shows that Fields had disguised the true identity of the author and was successful in masking himself as being the leader of the Farmer Organization.

In 1934, Congress passed the Bankhead Cotton Control Act. This act was aimed at controlling the amount of cotton produced in the United States, and Fields was not happy with what this meant to the rural South. The bill called for a 50 percent prohibitive tax, or at least five cents a pound, on cotton ginned in excess of the individuals' quota. If a farmer had a successful year and his neighbors had poor years, the successful farmer would have to pay a tax, or penalty as Fields would think, even though the producing area had below-average results.

Fields worked to get the bill repealed and had communication with several members of Congress outside the state of Louisiana.

Farmerville, Louisiana.
September 4th, 1934.

Dear Sir:

         As Secretary of the Farmer's Mass Meeting held at the Court House, September 1st, 1934, with reference to Federal Land Bank seizures, I herewith transmit a copy of the resolution passed unanimously by five hundred farmers, represented later through a committee of twenty, whose names appear signed below.

         Asking your consideration of the matter, and with kindest regards, I am

                    Yours very truly,

                         Mrs. Rosa Lee Forman
                              Secretary

Copy sent to:

Secretary Henry A. Wallace, Washington, D. C.
Congressman Riley J. Wilson, Ruston, La.
Sen. John H. Overton, Alexandria, La.
Pres. Franklin D. Roosevelt, Washington, D. C.
Senator Huey P. Long, Baton Rouge, La.
Federal Land Bank, New Orleans, La.

(copy)

Farmerville, Louisiana.
October 2nd, 1934.

United States Senator Smith,
Washington, D. C.

Dear Sir:-

I am glad to see that you are in favor of
changing the Bankhead Bill. You are on the right
track and the majority of the farmers are with you.

At the time the Bankhead Bill was passed
it looked to be a good remedy, but conditions arose
that changed the situation and that it should be
amended, modified or suspended, and is now proving
a curse to thousands of poor farmers in Louisiana,
Mississippi, Arkansas and Alabama. We hope you win.

Yours respectfully,

Harvey G. Fields, Chairman
Ouachita Valley Farm Relief
Committee.

HGF/hnm....

c c: J. H. Jones, Bonita, La.
     J. H. McClanahan, Columbia, La.
     W. R. Guess, Quitman, La.
     Sen. C. C. Brooks, St. Joseph, La.
     C. H. McKenzie, Monroe, La.
     F. A. Frye, Baton Rouge, La.

LOUISIANA PUBLIC SERVICE COMMISSION

HARVEY G. FIELDS, CHAIRMAN
   FARMERVILLE, LA.
WADE O. MARTIN,
   ST. MARTINVILLE, LA.
FRANCIS WILLIAMS,
   NEW ORLEANS, LA.

BATON ROUGE

P. A. FRYE, SECRETARY
   BATON ROUGE, LA.
ALEX GROUCHY,
   ASST. SECTY. AND GEN. FIELD AGENT

IN REPLY PLEASE REFER
TO OUR FILE NO.

Farmerville, Louisiana,
September 20th, 1934.

Mr. T. H. McGregor,
Member of House,
Austin, Texas.

My Dear Sir:—

    I want to congratulate you on your brave
and fearless fight against the use of the Bankhead
Bill at present.

    Thousands of Louisianians see it just as
you do and join you in your protest.

    The people are beginning to wake up, they
have caught on to the fact that there is too much
red tape, bureau work, and bosses over them, besides
the work of the theoretical brain trusters.

    I am wondering whether you are the T. H.
McGregor who use to live in Shreveport and was
engaged in business there as land agent for one of
the companies.

    Trusting and hoping that you win out in
your fight, I am

                Yours very truly,

                Harvey G. Fields, Chairman
             Ouachita Valley Farm Relief Committee.

HGF/hm....

The bill was eventually replaced following an appeal to the United States Supreme Court.

On August 9, 1935, President Roosevelt signed the Federal Motor Carrier Act. This act regulated interstate transport of passenger and property with the exception of livestock, fish, or agricultural commodities. One year earlier, the Louisiana legislature proposed a similar law for the state. This bill would require a state constitutional amendment to enact this act. The state legislature's Judiciary B Committee held the hearing in the Louisiana State Capital. Fields was concerned that he was not fully versed on the important legislation, that amendments had changed the bill in a negative manner, and he wasn't going to be pushed into agreeing with the bill to meet a scheduled date for submittal to the House for a vote. The committee wanted his endorsement before sending it to the House for a vote.

Several days before the Bill went to the committee in Baton Rouge, Fields met with members of the motor carrier organizations inside the state. He wanted to understand their stand and he also wanted to be sure that the bill was fair to all motor carrier operators in the state and did not favor an elite few. He called a confidential meeting at his home in Farmerville to discuss the bill. A copy of an invitation follows.

Farmerville, Louisiana.
June 1st, 1934.

Mr. W.M. Carnahan,
Alexandria, La.

Confidential:

Dear Sir:-

I do not like the looks of the Motor Bill in its present shape. If they would change it around and take some of the defects out I might be for it. It is too one-sided. I believe in seeing all people get the same kind of a square deal.

If you boys want to fight it and win out it had better be done in the next few days. I am suggesting that you come up and see me Sunday afternoon. If you will come here about 4 o'clock you could come up to my home and we will go over the matter and you could spend an hour with me and formulate plans for the correction of this bill. Do not give out anything public about me, as I prefer making my own statement about my position. I think you and I can go over the matter and plan a successful fight.

Yours very truly,

Harvey G. Fields.

HGF/m.

He had sent a letter to the committee stating his objections. This led to a letter to Fields from the nonlegislative author of the bill. Fields quickly responded, making it very clear that he would not be pressured into making a decision on such an important piece of legislation.

LOUISIANA PUBLIC SERVICE COMMISSION

HARVEY G. FIELDS, CHAIRMAN
FARMERVILLE, LA.

WADE O. MARTIN,
ST. MARTINVILLE, LA.

FRANCIS WILLIAMS,
NEW ORLEANS, LA.

BATON ROUGE

P. A. FRYE, SECRETARY
BATON ROUGE, LA.

ALEX GROUCHY,
ASST. SECTY. AND GEN. FIELD AGENT

IN REPLY PLEASE REFER
TO OUR FILE NO.

Farmerville, Louisiana
June 11th, 1934.

Mr. Fred G. Hudson,
Room 543,
Heidelberg Hotel,
Baton Rouge,
Louisiana.

Dear Fred:-

Your letter of the 8th received, and beg to say I have not made up my mind that I am entirely favorable to the Motor Carrier Act, as proposed, but I am very much more disposed to favor it than I was before it was changed and amended, which changes meet some of the very objections that I raised.

Frankly you charge that you have felt my attitude was unfair. I would not be afraid any day to compare my record with yours or anybody else's fairness, as I think the comparison would show that I have done about one hundred things for the people of this State to where you have done one. I gave you a polite hearing, but never did attempt to lead you to believe that I wouldaccept the Bill unless I felt it was a sound and fair measure. Of course I will admit it is a fairer measure then the 1932 measure you sponsored, which was criticized, and brought harsh excoriations from all other Louisiana, particularly from all of the motor operators, including the five or six, who are now cooperating with you, because I heard them cuss you and the Missouri Pacific good and strong, and so I think I fully understand the situation. My failure to reply to you was not intentional, as I am always exceedingly fair, but I have been crowded with other matters and did try to find you at Baton Rouge without any success.

Answering your letter paragraph by paragraph, and reaching paragraph four, I desire to say that I do not think you understand your own Bill, very much in the attitude of a mutual friend of ours, and I was in no sense wrong in my assumptions, so when you say I was inaccurate and unfair I want

#2--------FGH

to say that you are absolutely in error and your statements are
without any accuracy or correctness whatsoever. Now as to the
fact that Commissioners Williams and Martin see the thing different, and your statement that my position is unjust tomthem, why
that is ridiculous, as both of these gentlemen are entitled to
their opinion and i am entitled to mine. Commissioner Williams
and i have been together six years and we have voted practically
ninety percent together, when we differ both of us have such a
high respect for each other that we never stop to think anything
about it except that each man is following his own conscience
and judgment. Commissioner Martin has been on two years, and
I feel quite sure that he and i entertain exactly the same
feeling and spirit. i regard both of them as sincere in their
own acts, and i know I am in the same position, we are all
friends, and we follow our own heads and hearts.

        As to the damage done i think you are in for a fight and
your Bill is by no means passed, and when passed you will have
to go before the Bar of Public Opinion, and bear in mind that
thousands of those who determine the matter are just as intelligent
as we are, though some lawyers get egotistical now and then and
think they are the whole cheese.

        i think the private operators, farmers and taxicab men
will get a square deal. Their efforts will be protected by
those who have their cause at heart.

        One of the outstanding Members of the Committee that
passed on your Bill, who voted for a favorable report has written
me as follows: "Of course, there have been a number of amendments
offered which exempt various classes, but even with these
amendments i believe that the Bill is _bad_ because it goes much
further than regulation. In my humble opinion, it is purely and
simply a railroad measure, deliberately designed toddrive the
small man out of business because he has become a competitive
factor." This comes from an outstanding lawyer in Louisiana,who
voted to let your Bill go to the floor. I think you will find
other members of the Committee in the same shape.

```
#3.........FGH.


         In deference to Commissioner Martin, for whom I
entertain the very kindest of feelings, i am today taking
this Bill to Shreveport in accordance with my statement to
him, to study it with fair lawyers, who do not represent
interests, or who are not lobbyists, and see if we cannot work
out some amendment that will give the people a square deal
on the question of contracts, as the clause in this bill is
the most ambiguous expression i ever saw in a proposed bill.

         Trusting this answers in proper detail your letter,
and with my most kindest regards,

         i am

                    Yours very truly,


HGF/mm...                              Harvey G. Fields.


CC/ Mr. Wade Martin, St. Martinville, La.
    Mr. Francis Williams, New Orleans, La.
    Mr. P. A. Frye, Secy. Com. Baton Rouge, La.
    Mr. N. E. Dawson, Monroe, La.
    Mr. Joe Herrin, Alexandria, La.
    Mr. W. N. Carnahan, Alexandria, La.
    Mr. Joe Campbell, Shreveport, La.
    Mr. L. W. Baldwin, Pres. Mo. Pac. Monroe, La.
    Mr. R. Wynne, Alexandria, La.
    Mr. George Montague, New Orleans, La.
    Mr. W. K. Henderson, Shreveport, La.
    Mr. C. A. Riddle, Baton Rouge, Louisiana.
    Mr. Robt. D. Jones, Baton Rouge, La.
    Mr. W. J. Hammons, Baton Rouge, La.
    Mr. Ashley Wright, Baton Rouge, La.
    Mr. Carl Henry, Natchitoches, La.
    Col. R. W. J. Flynn, T.M., Standard Oil Co., New Orleans, La.
    Mr. O. L. Biedenharn, Shreveport, La.
    Mr. Lamar Polk, Alexandria, La.
    Mr. Jim Horton, Coushatta, La.
    Mr. Fred Heintz, Covington, La.
```

Changes were made, and a meeting was held that clarified the new bill. Fields did approve the measure following changes, the bill was passed, and the legislation was put into affect.

COCA-COLA BOTTLING COMPANY

OFFICE & FACTORY: 212 MARKET ST.

SHREVEPORT, LA.
June 22, 1934.

OFFICE OF
O. L. BIEDENHARN
Sect'y-Treas.

Hon. Harvey G. Fields,
La. Public Service Commission,
Baton Rouge, La.

Dear Mr. Fields:

I have copy of your letter of the 11th to Mr. Fred G.
Hudson and notice that quite a number of other gentlemen have also received a copy of this letter.

I have been out of the city for the past week is the
reason for delay in writing you.

I appreciate knowing your position with regard the
bill in question. I am wondering just why this copy
was sent me, hence this letter.

The bill originally drawn took the private carrier
under the Public Service Commission and, naturally, I
and my colleagues became interested. When the private
carrier was eliminated my position from then on was
neither for nor against the bill, leaving it entirely
up to the interests involved to thrash the bill out.
This so you may know definitely from me my position.

With best wishes and regards, I am

Yours sincerely,

OLB:C

Fields had also contacted various carriers that could be impacted if the laws were enacted. One of these was Coca-Cola. The first bottled Coke was in Monroe, Louisiana; and an executive of Coca-Cola was O. L. Biedenhorn, from the family that owned the bottling company. A copy of a letter from Biednharn to Fields follows that discloses that Fields had taken the fight for the common carrier to individuals that could have been impacted by the passage of an ill-prepared legislative bill.

Fields wasn't a person that was so mesmerized by Huey Long that he blindly followed his doctrines. As he stated on several occasions, he was independent and was his own man. When someone asked for a favor, he would ask, "Is he a good man, and did he support me in the past? As important as it is to help someone that has been my supporter in the past, I can look past that. The most important thing is that the person is a good man."

In California, a movement was started by longtime socialist Upton Sinclair. Just as in the 2009 recession, California was the personification of state financial problems. Massive unemployment, plant closures, foreclosures, and despair were rampant in California. Freight trains would be stopped at the state line, and people trying to get to California to get a job harvesting crops were not allowed to enter. Sinclair's motto was "End poverty in California." The acronym *EPIC* was showing up across the state. Sinclair had decided it was time to run for governor.

Upton Sinclair

DEMOCRATIC CANDIDATE FOR GOVERNOR!

IT'S UP TO YOU

How much MORE POVERTY do you want?
How much more UNCERTAINTY FEAR, HUNGER, PRIVATION, for YOURSELF,
    your FAMILY, your FRIENDS?
RICH OR POOR, YOU HAVE NO SECURITY.
If you are poor, you may be in the bread line, sleeping in Missions or under bridges.
If you are rich, you know not when ANOTHER crash may take your stocks and
    bonds, your business, your home, and put YOU among the down-and-outs!
CAN WE END POVERTY? CAN WE SAVE DEMOCRACY?
CAN WE EMPLOY THE UNEMPLOYED?
CAN WE SOLVE OUR PRESENT PROBLEMS WITHOUT A VIOLENT REVOLU-
    TION? The answer is YES!
We CAN end POVERTY. We CAN save DEMOCRACY.
We CAN employ the UNEMPLOYED. We CAN avert violent revolution.
As President Roosevelt's Recovery Program gains momentum the people of Cali-
    fornia are necessarily called on to retire the old-line politicians.
We have plenty of idle factories, plenty of idle land, and plenty of idle people. Then
    ALL WE NEED TO DO is to put the idle people to work in the idle factories
    and on the idle land, producing their own food clothing and shelter, for
    their own benefit and profit.
Just as SIMPLE as that. A ten-year-old child can understand it, and the people of
    California can do it whenever they get ready.
We are calling upon YOU—regardless of age, race, or creed—to join with us to put
    Upton Sinclair's EPIC PLAN into operation. He calls it the EPIC PLAN
    after the first letters of the words: END POVERTY IN CALIFORNIA!
For thirty years Upton Sinclair's first thought has been the WELFARE OF THHE
    COMMON PEOPLE!
SUPPORT HIM FOR GOVERNOR.
Register NOW as a DEMOCRAT. Join the Democratic Club in your District. Then
    in August go to the Polls and nomminate HIM. He is a sure winner and will
    bring the NEW DEAL nearer to Californians. His EPIC PLAN dove-tails
    nicely with the President's Recovery Program.
Let's be the first State to get out of the RED.
If Sinclair becomes our Governor THE UNEMPLOYED WILL NO LONGER BE
    PAUPERS—AND THE WILL NO LONGER RIDE ON THE BACKS OF THE
    TAX-PAYERS.
    Read the principal features of the EPIC PLAN on the reverse side of this
sheet. Or, better still, secure a copy of Sinclair's pamphlet—
    "I, Governor, and How I Ended Poverty In California."
REMEMBER—Register Democratic before July 19 and vote for Upton Sinclair.

UPTON SINCLAIR HEADQUARTERS

68 Haight Street, near Market, San Francisco
Phone HEmlock 6918

Printing Free by Cooperative Labor

Price 2 cents

Fields wanted to learn more of Sinclair's views, and he wrote him, requesting information about his philosophy.

Farmerville, Louisiana.
August 29th, 1934.

Mr. Upton Sinclar,
San Francisco, Calif.

Dear Mr. Sinclar:-
            I am interested in reading some of
your latest works and will ask you to please send me
a list of your latest books and the name of the
Publishing Company which handles them.

                        Yours very truly,

                        Harvey G.Fields.

HGF/m.

Sinclair did respond to the request and provided several speeches. These probably became too controversial for Fields as there was no other communication from Fields. Sinclair did well in the California gubernatorial primary but ultimately lost his bid for governor.

Fields was distressed with the increased plight of the farmers of the South. The farmers were having to fight the economic destruction of the Great Depression, the bureaucratic red tape of the federal governmental programs, and now a devastating drought. In 1934, he sent a letter to the secretary of agriculture requesting help for the farmers that were now in the middle of the drought.

Jonesboro, Louisiana.
Saturday, September 8th, 1934.

To the Honorable Secretary of Agriculture,
Washington, D. C.

To the Farm Credit Administration,
Washington, D. C.

Whereas, the Parish of Jackson, State of Louisiana, has a
large number of farmers who are financially depressed whose homes
are under mortgage, and who have been deprived of the benefit of
producing corn, and sufficient feed stuff necessary for raising of
cattle, hogs and fowls for sale, or for domestic use by the drouth
and dry spell, which has been in effect in this area for several
months; and,

Whereas, the lack of rain and showers in the Parish of
Jackson has greatly reduced our corn and cotton crops, our farmers
and land owners are in distress, with many of the necessities of
life costing much more than the prices of twelve months ago, with
the prices of cotton pegged below a price necessary to meet the
prices of other products, with many of our farmers and land owners
unable to meet their just debts, to pay their taxes, and without
sufficient assistance from the Relief Organization from the parish
and the State;

Be it Now Known, that we the farmers and land owners of
Jackson Parish, signers of this declaration and this petition
representing the sentiments and the condition of thousands of
others in this area, who are in the same position, do now petition
the Farm Loan Credit Administration, and Your Honorable Secretary of
Agriculture, to grant our people proper and early relief, and to
place this parish upon that classification which will secure
sufficient, immediate and proper benefits and assistance.

We declare that the citizens of this parish are a patriotic
and energetic people, who regret to ask for help, relief or work,
but whose financial condition is serious and precarious and who
are facing a more serious condition this approaching winter, and
we declare that those whose cause we are now pleading are with us
admirers and workers in the great cause, efforts and undertakings
of our Great Leader of the Nation at Washington.

We now respectfully ask Your Department and all other
Departments who have under their supervision the granting of
Drouth Relief and assistance to the land owners of this country
that they give to this area in its distress conditions the relief
and assistance intended by the President of the United States for
our farmers and home owners, which in many instances has not been
administered as he so intended, and we further ask that our
Congressman and Our Senators help as to secure this assistance.

Respectfully submitted.

Harvey Fields, Chairman Ouachita Valley
                    Farm Relief Committee.
W. R. Guess, Chairman, Jackson Parish
                    Drouth Relief Committee.
W. R. Kirbow
L. D. Ricks
N. W. McDow
Elzie Mazie
W. O. Lowe
Abe Salsburry
Ben Malone
Riley Leonard
A. D. Leonard

While Fields was addressing the plight of the farmer, studying Upton Sinclair, preparing for the vote on the Motor Carrier Act, and practicing law, Huey Long was making himself a common name across America. He launched two initiatives that would shake the very structure of the Democratic Party. First, he unveiled his Share Our Wealth doctrine. Second, he changed his newspaper from the *Louisiana Progress* to the *American Progress* and began nationwide distribution. He would now impose his beliefs on a nation and not just on a state.

Long proposed a set of taxes that would distribute wealth across the country. The wealthy would be taxed on wealth at the rate of 1 percent above one million dollars, 2 percent above two million dollars, 4 percent for the fourth million, 8 percent for the fifth million, 16 percent for the sixth million, 32 percent for the seventh million, 64 percent for the eighth million, and 100 percent for anything greater. Also, the income tax would be 100 percent if over one million dollars.

The Senate would not approve any of his programs, and he burst into a tirade on the Senate floor and proclaimed, "A mob is coming to the other ninety-five of you, damn scoundrels, and I'm undecided whether to stick here with you or go out and lead them."

Long then launched his Share the Wealth Society and had Reverend Gerald Smith organize the local clubs.

The Share the Wealth doctrine called for the following:

1. No person would be allowed to accumulate a personal net worth of more than one hundred to three hundred times the average family value. In 1932, this equated to a cap of one and a half to five million dollars.
2. Every family would receive with a homestead allowance of not less than one-third the average family wealth.
3. An old-age pension would be provided for anyone over age sixty.
4. The government would store surplus and would not destroy crops as were being done in 1932. The destruction of crops was a major concern of Fields's.
5. Veterans were paid what they were owed. This too was a pet peeve of Fields's as many of the veterans were provided with compensation when they returned from active service.
6. There would be equal opportunity for all children to receive an education.
7. Revenue to support the programs would come from the rich at the top of the scale.

True to Long's methods to sell an ideal, a large paper identifying the virtues of the society and the ills of the Democratic Party was widely distributed across the country.

(Reprint from Congressional Record—not printed at Government Expense)

PEOPLE OF AMERICA :—

In every community get together at once and organize a:

SHARE OUR WEALTH SOCIETY

MOTTO:

EVERY MAN A KING

Additionally, small flyers were passed out to the multitude that proclaimed what a Share the Wealth Society would do for education.

EDUCATIONAL PROGRAM

FOR SHARE OUR WEALTH SOCIETY

Government Assumes the Cost and Burden to Guarantee College, Professional, and Vocational Education to All Students

Under the present policy of government the young man and young woman whose parents are possessed of means can be given a college education or vocational and professional training. There are some exceptions to this rule; that is to say, that in some few cases students can find work by which to pay their expenses through college. As a general rule, however, only those with parents possessing extraordinary means can attend college.

"All men are created equal," says the Declaration of Independence, and to all those born the constitution of our Nation guarantees "life, liberty, and the pursuit of happiness."

These provisions of our immortal national documents are not observed when the right to education rests upon the financial ability of one's parents rather than upon the mental capacity of a student to learn and his energy to apply himself to the proper study necessary for him to learn.

The "share our wealth" program contemplates that from the billions of excess revenue brought into the United States Treasury by limiting fortunes to a few million dollars to any one person, that such large sums will be expended by the Government as will afford college education and professional training to all students based upon their mental capacity and energy rather than upon the wealth of their parents. Such an education contemplates not only the scholarship but such supplies and living costs as a student may have in order to attend college.

This will transfer the youth of our land into making preparation for building a better and greater nation. It will take their surplus labor out of the ranks of employment and afford more room for others; it will mean an immediate expansion of our educational facilities and the bringing back into active service of hundreds of thousands of learned instructors whose intellect and capacities, now idle, may be used for the moral, spiritual, and intellectual uplift of the Nation. Architects, engineers, builders, material men, and craftsmen now idle would find extensive and continued field for employment in providing and maintaining such extended educational facilities in the Nation.

All in all, the program is one of national organization; it means no great or burdensome outlay because there is a surplus of the goods and things needed for the care of all students, and the consuming of the same will immediately aid our problems of overproduction.

HUEY P. LONG,
United States Senator.

(Reprinted from Congressional Record, February 1, 1935)

United States Senate

COMMITTEE ON THE JUDICIARY

Dear Friend:-

Your letter received. Just as soon as we can, we will make an answer to any specific question you ask. Our letters are arriving by the thousands at a time and with our limited funds we work night and day to answer them as fast as we can.

However, for the present, we must hurry the work of every community in organizing a Share Our Wealth Society. Therefore we are answering you immediately by sending the general circular on how to proceed to organize a society, which circular describes our program in general detail. It is important that when you have organized such society for one community, or part of one community, that some committee or person should be named to get around into all nearby sections to get them to organize societies there.

As soon as you have organized your society and notified us about it, we will send you such copies of other bulletins and speeches as you may need and also books and manuals so that you can proceed on all fronts.

But the immediate necessity is to hurry to get our people busy in the work. If you knew how much that the fact these societies are organizing everywhere is causing the politicians to yield here and there already, you would appreciate how absolutely necessary to our purpose it is that we get the people into a society so that they may meet and become informed, thereafter to proceed along intelligent and unified lines.

Please hurry with the work to get your society organized. Write me as soon as you have completed organization. Be sure to send in the coupon off of the circular with the names of your officers.

Yours sincerely,

HPL/EJC   U. S. Senator.

Fields had lost all confidence in the congressional leadership in North Louisiana as it pertained to the support for the farmers and landowners in their time of greatest need. Fields wasn't backing a specific candidate for the position of congressman, but he definitely was politicking against one candidate. Riley Wilson was in Fields's sights, and Fields was relentless in his attacks. Eventually, Wilson was defeated and was replaced by Newt Mills.

```
                    NOTICE OF PUBLIC MEETING

              SATURDAY NIGHT, 7:30 P.M. AFTER SUPPER

ON SATURDAY, SEPTEMBER 8th, 1934, at the Court House, Jonesboro,
Louisiana, 7:30 PM several candidates for Congress will discuss vital
issues of the day with the voters of Jackson Parish.

Farm Relief, Drouth Relief, Flood Relief, Economy, Soldiers Bonus,
and many important questions will be discussed in detail by able and
capable speakers.

WHY the farmers did not get all the help they should have gotten.

WHY the soldier boys were refused help and got no money, when many
of them were injured, gassed and maimed, will be explained.

WHY the ERA help did not benefit all the farmers will be carefully
explained.

WHY Wilson played with the politicians instead of the farmers will
be thoroughly explained to your satisfaction.

WHY Wall Street wins and the poor people lost will be made a special
topic of the day.

HOW Mrs. Kemp got stabbed in the back, and who did it will be thorough-
ly, clearly and in vivid language explained to the voters of this
District.

We need more help for the farmer. We need drouth relief and we need
to stop the sale of farmers homes by the Federal Land Bank during the
worst days of the depression. Bread and meat may be scarce for some
poor boys in Jackson this winter. Come out and help us fill the
dinner pail.

Come out and bring plenty more people with you. Tell your neighbor
about it and do not fail to show up at the Court House Saturday NIGHT
afternoon SEPTEMBER 8th, 1934.

                              Independent Voters and Supporters
                              of McKenzie, Harper and Mills.
```

Fields also well understood the power of the press. He also realized that people tired of hearing from a lone crusader, even if the crusader was right and just in his cause. Fields would use his journalistic ability by submitting letters to newspapers unsigned. The following illustrates this. It was not his first time to do so, nor would it be his last.

Monroe, Louisiana,
June 30th, 1934.

CLEAN OUT SOME OF OUR POLITICAL HOUSES AND TURN OUT
THOSE WHO HAVE FORGOTTEN THE TOILING FARMERS AND THE BUDDIES WHO FOUGHT
THE WAR WHILE POLITICIANS AND MILLIONAIRES PROFITEERED.

The time to elect congressmen again has rolled around. Mr.
Voter, it is time to think before we make up our minds as to who is the
man to supplant Mr. Riley Joe Wilson in congress, after his twenty years
of fun, leisure and drawing of salaries and expenses amounting to two
hundred twenty-five thousand dollars, NEARLY A QUARTER OF A MILLION
DOLLARS donated to the affable congressman.

The farmers need help, have had to cope with serious problems,
yet in trouble, without any effort or result from our congressman, but
only receiving aid from others who did not owe the same duty to the
landowners of this section.

Veterans and ex-service boys had to wait two years longer on
account of Wilson and his gang who bucked and snorted and bellowed
before they took their orders from the folks at home. We need a change,
twenty years of fun is enough for any good man. We cannot afford to
spend our money on sideshows while farmers, laborers and crippled
soldiers and their families are suffering for food and clothing.
Wake up Mr. Farmer, think what has happened and what more is to happen
before you vote. Attention Mr. Ex-Service Man. Think before you vote.
Check the record of Riley J. Wilson and then do your duty.

Mr. Laborer, before you begin the days work pause and think about
it. Compare Wilson's sympathy for labor with that of McKenzie who risked
his life for his country, with Harper who has always been considered a
poor man's friend, with Mills who advocated more for the poor and needy,
with Andrews who is a farmers friend, or Clark who never acts the
hypocrite, but known for his extreme sincerity, then decide whether you
will keep in office the wealthy congressman who now occupies the seat
from the fifth district. Do not take orders from other gang. Vote an
honest vote and let the little politicians fight among themselves. A
vote for Wilson is a vote against labor, farmer, war buddies, for the
great and powerful rich against the poor and weak. A vote for Wilson
is a vote to keep in Republican Postmasters, Republican Marshalls,
as they have been kept in while Democrats who need jobs have suffered
and sucked their thumbs for nourishment. A vote for Wilson means a
life time cinch on the office with no chance for young men or new
blood in office. A vote for Wilson means politicians, job traders
and E.R.A. managers in several parishes where the farmers have been
slapped in the face and deprived of work with no help from Wilson will
continue their political exploitations.

A vote for McKenzie, Harper, Mills, Clark or Andrews means a
vote for progress, clean politics, assistance to the farmers a square
deal to war buddies and to the hardworking laborers of our country.

(Signed) A Group of War Buddies-Plain
Farmers and Laborers of the
Fifth District.

Fields was every bit as sensitive to the plight of the American serviceman as he was to the citizen that was suffering from class distinction and economic disparity. Often he would voice complaints that the "boys" that so valiantly had served the United States had then been forgotten. He felt that they deserved the support and respect from the government that they had served and a nation they had protected.

Ironically, as staunch a supporter of Long as Fields was and as much as Long was despised by the Roosevelt administration, Fields was being considered for a position within the federal government. This lends some evidence that Fields was identified as an individual and not merely a member of the Long political machine. Fields also realized that endorsements help get an individual placed in a political position.

Farmerville, Louisiana,
August 30th, 1935.

Professor H.L.Noble,
Gibsland, Louisiana.

My dear Friend:-
       Inasmuch as my name may be submitted
President Roosevelt and to the Louisiana Delegation
for Federal Attorney of Louisiana, or along some other
line, I am taking the liberty of sending you a few
blank letters, addressed to your Congressman, and to
ask you if you can get Williams, Mr. Houck and several
Members of your Council, together with yourself, I
would appreciate your having them signed and returning
them to your Congressman. Also write me who signed
so I can have a record of what my friends have done.

       I am enclosing a stamped envelope for
the Congressman and myself. If you and Williams can
sign at once please send the letters to Washington right
away. I have about as good a chance as anybody right
today. Do not give out to the press.

      With best regards,

                Your friend,

                Harvey Fields.

HGW/m.

encls....

Long's Share the Wealth Society had swelled to twenty-seven thousand clubs, which bragged about a membership of 7.5 million, and Long's Senate office was receiving as many as sixty thousand letters a week. This swell of public approval caused a shift in the direction of the Roosevelt administration, and there was a move to the left. The second "New Deal" was launched and included the Social Security Act. Roosevelt did privately admit that he was trying to steal Long's thunder. The philosophical change was too late for Long, and many speculated that he would make a run for president in 1936.

One reason for the success of the Share the Wealth Society was the newspaper *American Progress*. Originally begun in Louisiana as the *Louisiana Progress*, this weekly paper explained what was happening in Washington and what the society could expect if Long was in power. The paper was selling hope. Prior to launching the paper, Fields was one of the recipients of a letter from Long that explained the new periodical, what it was to accomplish, and a subscription form to be used to sell the paper.

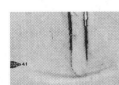

HUEY P. LONG
UNITED STATES SENATOR
NEW ORLEANS, LA.

July 5, 1933

Dear Friend:

We want to get out from Washington to our friends and
to the public generally all over the United States on the
important general issues of the day. Heretofore at the expense
of my friends and myself, I have sent out some of the speeches
I have made in the United States Senate; but the information
contained in them is meager and incomplete. The cost is more
than we can contribute much further.

Our first, last and principal fight has been to spread
the wealth of this land among all the people. In the land of too
much to eat and wear and too many houses, there is no explanation
for our hungry, naked and homeless people, except the greed of
the few whose wealth is more than they can use. It is a shame
on our civilization that one million people have more than they
can use if they live to be ten thousand years old, but that
119,000,000 people are becoming more and more destitute as times
pass. And yet we have permitted it, despite the Bible telling us
it must not be done and despite the warnings of all great men that
it would wreck the country and ruin our people. To break up such
a system was the object of many of us supporting our present
president.

But in this day and land of too much, the members of the
National Economy League, financed by a set of multi-millionaires,
have actually had their way in stripping down the salaries and
wages of public workers and in having the wounded and disabled
veterans of our wars given less than 1/2 the food and medicine
they need to live on. Some of them are to be given nothing at
all - so that the income and inheritance taxes on the big rich
estates should not be made heavier, as we have proposed so as to
decentralize wealth.

We have gained great headway in our move from the
standpoint of our liberal voting strength; our vote in Congress
has trebled, but the sinister interests are trying to make hay
while the sun shines. They are working fast enough in this

—2—

depression to squeeze out many of the home owners there are left
and to reduce their own taxes, if possible, by putting all taxes
on the struggling masses, or by cutting down the wage basis of
the man who works for a living. All this proposal for a sales
tax means that the 119,000,000 will pay 99% of it, whereas we
propose that such should be paid by the multi-rich 1% that owns
more than all the balance of the 119,000,000 people put together.

One of the first things we must try to do now, before
it is too late, is to save the system of community banks for the
people so that all resources of finance may not be more closely
tied up in a few hands. We must try to get help for the depositors
of closed banks and assure that the guarantee bank deposit law
will work for the future protection of everyone alike.

We must fight to avoid the country being opened up on
a basis of mere economic slavery for the masses, with the ruling
classes greater in power and standing than ever. That is usually
how depressions end, the rich become richer and the poor become
poorer. A great talk today is that if the people generally have
an assurance of something to eat and wear and any kind of a place
to live in, they should be satisfied. Some seem to think that the
holders of big fortunes are kind to let the sun shine on us. They
seem to be spoken of as the divine set to handle the Lord's bless-
ings on earth, and as generous to allow some of us nondescript
and accidental 119,000,000 people to have more and some less.
They speak as though the world owes its existence to the rulers
of money and finance, whereas the truth is, it is capital demanding
and receiving an unscrupulous return that has robbed the masses
of the fruits of their earnings to bring almost the whole population
where it has no power to buy and the country where it is today
as a result.

We are getting out a newspaper, "The American Progress",
to be published every week, giving the fair side of the news and
the issues of the day. We expect to make this paper one of
general information on all vital issues to the people, written in
such a way that it can be understood. Our great trouble in America
today is the ignorance of our people, even our most prominent
citizens, in the affairs of our country. Help us to get this
paper in the hands of the people to be read. We can send this
to each subscriber for 50¢ per year. The postal regulations will
only let us send it out to bona fide subscribers. Money contributed
to help the paper will not help us. We need you to get us as
many subscribers as you can and forward them to us as quick as
possible so we can get going. I enclose you a list on which to
write the names of subscribers. Just get us as many as you can

—3—

and don't forget to include your own in the list. We will publish the paper here from New Orleans for a few weeks, after which we expect to publish it from Washington, D. C. Write us as quickly as possible if you can help us out and how much you can do toward getting us subscribers. We do not want you or anyone else to send a single dollar to help the paper except by giving the name of the subscribers and sending us 50¢ for each of them.

We will greatly appreciate your help to carry on the very best fight we can make at all times for the general welfare of all the people of this nation. And we assure you our publication will contain only facts which no one can or will dispute, but such facts as are seldom, if ever, given to the people by some of our big publications. Please let us hear from you on how much you can help, if possible, in getting us subscribers, thereby obliging,

Yours sincerely,

Huey P. Long

P. S. Please send subscriptions and make checks payable to "THE AMERICAN PROGRESS", 822 Perdido Street, New Orleans, La.

H.P.L.

Let There Be Light — Live and Let Live

Subscribe to

The American Progress
" LET THE FUR FLY "
A WEEKLY NEWSPAPER SPONSORED by HUEY P. LONG
One Whole Year for 50c

*Would you like to see the unvarnished news
and the people's side of public questions?*

We propose to give a condensed story of the news, and to present the facts to show the underlying cause of human distress and business paralysis in America as seen and foreseen by every leading statesman of this and all other countries, and as warned against by the laws of the Lord.

With 1% of our people owning nearly twice as much as all the other 99%, how is a country ever to have permanent progress unless there is a correction of this evil?

We will show that there is not now, and never has been any cause for distress in America!

We will show that to have allowed people to starve in the land of plenty is a crime of a greed that must be held within limits to save our civilization.

Let There Be Light — Live and Let Live

The American Progress
" LET THE FUR FLY "
A WEEKLY NEWSPAPER SPONSORED by HUEY P. LONG

50c Per Year   New Orleans, La.

*Note: In the near future we propose to publish THE AMERICAN PROGRESS
from Washington, D. C.*

FRANKLIN PTG. CO.   NEW ORLEANS, LA.

Long's rule over Louisiana was monumental. O. K. Allen was manipulated by Long to support any endeavor Huey desired. Long was writing legislation and making whirlwind trips to Louisiana from Washington to ensure the legislation was being passed. He called two special sessions, and although dictatorial in nature, his rule was paying dividends for the residents of Louisiana, and many were having some form of hope that they were no longer ignored. During his four years as governor, Louisiana went from 331 miles of paved roads to 2,301 miles, plus an additional 2,816 miles of gravel roads. By the beginning of 1936, the infrastructure programs he began had completed nine thousand miles of paved roads. The night schools he promised the residents of Louisiana taught one hundred thousand uneducated adults to read, and children were receiving free textbooks. He had the poll tax repealed in 1935, and thus, voter registration increases by 76 percent. Long also instituted a free-lunch program that would feed children from families that could not afford the school lunches. But Long still had many enemies, and some were bent on rescuing the state from this dictator.

Huey had called for a special session to be held, and obedient to his request, his colleagues called the special session. This was the third special session, and it was only July. Long traveled from Washington to Baton Rouge by train to be in attendance to ensure his legislation passed. Previously, a Judge Benjamin Henry Pavy had been gerrymandered out of his sixteenth judicial district, and the speculation was that it was due to his opposition to Long. Additionally, Pavy's daughter had been removed as a teacher at LSU, and it was believed that Long was behind this also. Fields later noted that it was a mistake for Long to have taken this action, and Long should not have listened to advisers pertaining to Pavy. Fields also noted that Pavy was an honorable and capable judge.

On September 8, 1935, Huey Long was entering the corridor near the House of Representatives at the Louisiana State Capital. His bodyguards trailed behind him. Suddenly Dr. Carl Weiss, husband of the terminated teacher and son-in-law of Judge Pavy, stepped out, pulled out a pistol, and shot Huey once. Weiss was immediately riddled with sixty-one bullets from the bodyguards and police behind the senator.

Long was taken to the Lady of the Lake hospital next to the capital, where he lingered for two days. During the time that Long was in his room, a very small select group of individuals were allowed in. Among these were his wife; his three brothers; Governor O. K. Allen; Seymour Weiss, Fields's close friend and confidant; Lieutenant Governor James A. Noe; a special nurse; Dr. Arthur Vidrine, who was head of New Orleans Charity Hospital; Dr. J. Q. Graves from Monroe; and Dr. E. L. Sanderson of Shreveport.

Long never passed the reins of control to anyone while in the hospital. Allen and Weiss both pushed to get the keys to the famous deduct box that contained political and other legal papers. He refused until he realized that he might not survive and then gave up the keys. It was later said that the box was discovered and was found to be empty.

Fields was also told that Long said, "I want to live and finish my work. I don't want to die now. There's so much more to be done." At one time, he said, "I love the boys and girls of LSU. I can't just leave them now."

One transfusion was given the senator, and this came directly from Jimmy Noe. As he was slipping in and out of consciousness, he was heard to mutter, "Oh God! My work is not finished. What will my poor university boys do without me?"

Huey Long drifted into death on September 10, 1935. His funeral was befitting a man that had spent his life wanting to help a state that so badly needed it. His casket was placed in the state capital. Over one hundred thousand mourners passed by to say good-bye to the man that gave them hope.

Long was interred on the capital grounds, and a spotlight from the top of the building he had constructed shines down on his statue. Almost before the services were over, the conspiracy theories began.

Fields uncovered three plots following the actual assassination. The first came from various leaders and was manifested from anger toward Long. According to Fields, the conspirators wore a piece of red ribbon to denote a type of brotherhood that was aligned in the assassination attempt. This was never manifested in any clear planning, and Fields spoke little about it.

The second attempt appears to have been better planned. Prior to the assassination, Fields was visiting Long in his hotel room and witnessed the presence of several armed bodyguards. Fields questioned Long about them and asked if he really thought that he was in peril. Long quickly answered that he was. He told Fields that there was a conspiracy for a cab to ram him between Baton Rouge and New Orleans. Fields discounted this as improbable since the cabdriver would have been committing suicide. Then several months after the assassination, it was revealed to Fields that this, in fact, had been the plot. The cabby would swerve at the car and jump after doing so. The reward was a large sum of money. The conspiracy was very detailed and called for several people to be along the route to report on the senator's movement. According to the report given to Fields, one man had a bout of conscience and confessed to a priest. The priest couldn't divulge the man's name but did pass on the plot details. A very prominent radio evangelist was informed of the plot and made the call to Long.

The third was the plot that actually led to the assassination. Dr. Weiss, in a fit of anger, succeeded in shooting and mortally wounding Huey Long. Fields did uncover several points that would lead one to suspect that there were others involved in the Long assassination. A week before the shooting, a wealthy banker was asked to drop into a hat a contribution to aid in the defense of an assailant to help the widow in case of his death. The banker refused. A national radio announcer had also heard of a plot. Whether the actual assassination was a part of the second plot that was mentioned or was an independent act will never be known. What is known is that two unidentified men were standing in the hall following the shooting and were never identified or seen again.

There were quite a lot of rumors about who actually killed Long. Some say that Weiss only hit Long with his fist, and a stray bullet from one of the bodyguards hit Huey. Fields performed his own investigation. One man on the scene was a former sheriff and state legislator by the name of J. E. Maclannahan from Caldwell Parish. He was present at the shooting and told Fields that he saw Weiss pull a gun and shoot Huey. Fields also talked to Sheriff Elliot Coleman, who was present at the shooting. He confirmed that Weiss pulled a gun and shot Long one time. No bodyguard's bullet hit Long.

Long's legacy was not what he had expected. He inherited a political scene that was full of corruption, and he left his kingdom to an organization that quickly forgot the causes their leader so embraced. Huey had stated that if he left his power in the hands of his lieutenants, they would all wind up in prison. Much of what he inherited and much of what happened after he left office had been identified as Long-inspired philosophy.

The speculation that Long would run for president in 1936 was unfounded. He did plan to form a third party and thus split the Democratic Party. He would select the candidate for his party, but it would not be him. This would lead to the downfall of the Democrats in the 1936 elections. In 1940, after the Republicans had a chance to fix the economy and failed, Long would run on his new party's ticket and rally enough Democrats to win.

This begs the question as to whether Long was the first to use this political tactic. In 1924 Al Smith was identified to be non-electable due to his Catholic religion. Nothing had changed by 1928 to make him anymore electable; however, Roosevelt became his campaign manager and successfully had him nominated. Four years later, Smith was abandoned by Roosevelt and following the collapse of the Hoover Administration, Roosevelt was elected and placed in office.

Following his death, Long's Share the Wealth started to come unraveled. Reverend Gerald Smith began to place his own beliefs into Share the Wealth, and ideals such as white supremacy soon led to the demise of Long's dream of a better life for the underprivileged.

Fields had lost a close friend and a crusader for the same causes that he was championing. He established a memorial service that was held in Farmerville and contacted Huey Long Sr., requesting that he attend. Dr. Smith and Governor Allen were scheduled to be in attendance. This letter follows.

HARVEY G. FIELDS,   H. B. CHAMBERS,   J. E. McCLANNAHAN
FARMERVILLE, LA.   MANGHAM, LA.   COLUMBIA, LA.
CHAIRMAN   VICE-CHAIRMAN   SECRETARY

FIFTH DEMOCRATIC CONGRESSIONAL COMMITTEE

Farmerville, _____ La.

October 14, 1935.

Mr. Huey P. Long, Sr.,
Winnfield, Lr.,

Dear Sir:-

Dr. Gerald Smith and probably Governor Allen will
be here Wednesday, October 23rd, at 2 P.M. in a Memorial
Service in honor of your distinguished son Senator Long, and
I have been asked to invite you to attend.

I wish you could come and if you say yes I will
send for you and you will make the trip at our expense.

It would be a great honor to have the father of
the most distinguished man in Louisiana and in the South
sit on the stage at our meeting. Let me know at once whether
you can come and do your best to say yes.

Your friend,

Harvey G. Fields.

HGF/m.

The Dr. Gerald Smith that is referenced in the letter was the theologian who gave the eulogy at Huey Long's funeral, and who also took control of the Share the Wealth Society.

Fields was deeply saddened by the death of his friend Huey Long, but continued with his legal profession while at the same time attacking the institutions and individuals that suppressed the working class of America.

In 1936, Harvey G. Fields was named Federal District Attorney for the Western District of Louisiana.

CHAPTER 6

RICHARD LECHE AND
THE LOUISIANA SCANDALS

$\mathbf{R}$ichard Leche was born in New Orleans on May 15, 1898. In 1916, when Harvey Fields was representing his North Louisiana district in the Louisiana senate, Richard "Dick" Leche entered Tulane University. When the United States entered World War I, Leche dropped out of Tulane and joined the U.S. Army, where he attained the rank of second lieutenant. After he was discharged from the army, he went to Chicago, where he made a living as an automobile-parts salesman. Soon after this, he was back in Louisiana, where he entered and graduated from Loyola University with a degree in law. Leche began his practice in 1923.

Five years after Leche started his legal practice, he ran for the Louisiana state senate. Even though he lost this bid for a public office, his quest for politics had just begun. In 1930, Governor Huey Pierce Long had welcomed him into the Long camp. Leche proceeded to successfully manage the Huey Long race for the United States Senate.

Fields surely had associations with Leche by 1930. Fields had been a law partner of the Long brothers and was now a member of the Public Service Commission. An insider in the Long administration, Fields would have had contacts with Huey's campaign manager.

Long left for Washington in 1932 to be sworn into the United State Senate. Huey had left Oscar K. "O. K." Allen back in Louisiana as the heir apparent to head the state. Huey had handpicked Allen to maintain Long's tight control on the state. Richard Leche, a climber in the Long organization, was selected by Long to be Allen's secretary. This appointment was due in part to the support provided by Leche to the Long campaign; however, Huey had ulterior motives. By having Leche close to Allen, Huey had a way to keep track of Allen's actions. This demonstrates the cautiously calculating demeanor of the Long administration as O. K. Allen was in fact a close friend of Long's and was raised in the same parish that was Long's home. There are stories that Leche sent weekly reports to Long in Washington.

Originally, Leche was reluctant to take the job when Long offered it. His law firm was doing quite well when the offer was made. Long promised in a middle-of-the-night meeting with Leche that he would increase the number of clients for Leche if he took the job. Leche accepted the secretarial job.

Long later repaid Leche's loyalty by getting Richard an appointment as an appeals court judge for Orleans Parish in 1934. This also continued to solidify Long's hold on the state. Such positions and paybacks were not uncommon in that period of time. It wasn't until the civil service laws of the Sam Jones administration were put into place in the early1940s that political appointees began to be replaced with individuals that were placed in positions based on testing and experience.

In the summer of 1935, the Huey Long political machine was solidly in control of the state of Louisiana. Huey was in the Senate in Washington and was a definite thorn in the side of President Franklin Roosevelt. Long's popularity with the common man in the middle of the Great Depression had Roosevelt worried. His power in Louisiana was absolute. Then on September 8, 1935, everything changed. Long was crossing the hall near what is now the House of Representative chambers in Baton Rouge, was shot, and later died from a bullet from the gun fired by Dr. Carl Weiss.

At the time of Huey's assassination, O. K. Allen was still in office as governor. Shortly before his term ended, Allen dropped dead in the governor's mansion. A brain hemorrhage abruptly ended the life of the man that had been chosen to replace Huey's Senate seat. James "Jimmy" A. Noe was next in line to be governor and assumed this position for the duration of Allen's term. In addition to being a politician in the Long powerhouse, he was a very successful businessman. Noe and Fields had been friends for years and continued to be until Fields's death.

After the loss of both Huey Long and O. K. Allen, the Long political machine was in a power vacuum and needed a candidate to inherit the reins of the state after the 1936 elections. Allen had already been selected to take the Senate post left open after Huey's assassination, and Allen was now gone.

The decision was made that Dick Leche would head the gubernatorial ticket and Earl Long, Huey's brother, would run for lieutenant governor. This decision came after a period of backroom politics that involved various members of the Long administration. Included in the negotiations were Robert Maestri, mayor of New Orleans; Governor O. K. Allen; Seymour Weiss, an architect; Abe Shushan; and the good friend of Fields and standing governor, James A. Noe.

Leche and Long ran against and defeated anti-Long candidate Cleveland Dear by a virtual landslide by running on the popularity of the Huey Long Share the Wealth doctrine. A large swearing-in ceremony was held. A gigantic mural of Huey Long was hung as a backdrop to the stands where the speeches were given, and Leche was presented to the state as the newest governor of Louisiana. The admiration and love for Huey was being exploited to play on the emotions of the Louisiana populace.

During the time that Leche was campaigning for and then elected to be the governor of Louisiana, Fields was being appointed by the attorney general of the United States to become the federal district attorney for the Western Region of Louisiana. Fields had campaigned for this position. Even though he had received correspondence requesting that he not leave the Public Service Commission, he felt that he personally needed a change. His belief was that he could make a bigger impact by becoming a federal prosecutor. In 1936, he received his appointment.

Huey had made the statement that if he didn't stay in control of Louisiana, members of his team would steal the place blind. Leche proved Long right and left no doubt about his intentions when he took office.

"When I took the oath of office, I didn't take any vow of poverty," Leche commented soon after he went into office.

Leche exhibited a lifestyle of massively brute beauty. This is exhibited in the house he constructed soon after taking office. Despite receiving a salary of $7,500 as the governor of Louisiana, he purchased approximately 1,200 acres on the Tchefuncte River. The value of this property was in the neighborhood of $20,000. Leche then proceeded to build a massive structure on his property. Nothing but the very best of materials was used. Unavailable today, the floors were made of heart-of-pine while the walls consisted of pecky cypress. There were reports that prisoners were used in the construction. A nine-acre lake was built and flooded from artesian wells. Stone came from as far away as Arkansas and Tennessee.

Dick Leche is credited with providing the basic layout sketches of the massive home. These sketches were presented to Leon C. Weiss, a successful architect who proceeded to produce the final design drawings.

Weiss and his firm provided financial backing of Huey Long in his successful run for governor in 1928 and later fought the Long impeachment attempt in 1929. Weiss later designed the majority of the monuments for the Long administration. His plans of the tallest state capital in the United States in Baton Rouge, the governor's mansion, buildings on the LSU campus and the LSU Medical Center in New Orleans made him a member of one of the most successful architectural firms in America. His link with members of the old Long regime continued after Huey's death. Weiss's designs delivered during the Dick Leche administration included various structures at LSU and the gigantic charity hospital in New Orleans. In 1939, Weiss was indicted with other members of the Leche administration. No other member of the successful architectural firm was indicted. Fields assembled many parts of the case for the government. Ironically, Weiss, who was one year older than Fields, attended Tulane's school of engineering, the same university that Fields received his law degree from, and was born and raised in rural Farmerville, Louisiana, the same rural town where Fields eventually married a native, set up his law practice, and lived out his life.

Richard Leche had run on Huey Long's Share the Wealth doctrine. Soon after taking office, this quickly changed as he embraced the Long-despised New Deal policies of Franklin Roosevelt. Leche played the political game well, and the rewards were soon being lavished on him from the administration in Washington.

While Huey Long was serving Louisiana in the U.S. Senate, he was proving to be a major headache for the Roosevelt administration. Long attacked the Roosevelt New

Deal policy as an attempt to discredit the policy and gain acceptance of his Share the Wealth program. Roosevelt's administration retaliated by beginning an investigation into the Long machine in Louisiana. There is one story that the decision was made to file charges against Long on income tax evasion on the day that he was assassinated. Roosevelt understood the strength of the Democratic Party in Louisiana and the impact it had on the national campaign. Fields was a major contributor to this success. His devotion to the party and his ties with national leaders of the Democratic Party helped solidify the state's position. Roosevelt also understood the threat that was being posed to him by the Long administration, so the investigations were launched. Fields was never a target of these investigations.

The investigation was a political tool that was in use at that time. An earlier investigation had been launched by the Hoover administration looking into the Long political machine. This investigation was squashed when the Democratic Roosevelt administration moved into the White House in 1932. It wasn't until Huey began his attacks that the investigations were renewed.

Dick Leche had been considered to be a dupe that was being manipulated by members of the late Huey Long's administration. Nothing could be farther from the truth. Leche was a successful lawyer and had been handpicked by Huey to be O. K. Allen's secretary. Long selected positions based on both loyalty and the ability to perform the work. Leche's creativity is demonstrated in his initial design of his masculine home and surrounding landscaped properties.

He also had a knack for identifying an opportunity and responding to its implementation immediately. This was demonstrated when he saw a photo shoot to promote Louisiana products. When Leche observed a young lady being photographed in a rice costume, he immediately jumped up and proclaimed that the state should have a rice festival. Within minutes, Leche's excitement was at a frenzy, and various state officials were moving to make the festival happen. Crowley, Louisiana, was selected to host the festival; and following a marketing blitz in the Deep South, the LSU marching band and cheerleaders kicked off the festival. Ironically, Crowley is the home of Edwin Edwards, the second Louisiana governor to be indicted and sent to federal prison.

As adept as he was at viewing potential opportunities and working within the political system, his loyalty to the Long doctrine of Share the Wealth that propelled him into office was not as important as the personal gains that were available to him and his supporters. Leche realized that he had to change his position if he was to gain the success he desired.

Leche dropped his Share the Wealth doctrine that he inherited from the Long faction. His new praise and support of the Roosevelt New Deal policy brought newfound wealth to both Louisiana and the Leche administration. So immense was the funds flowing into Louisiana that the term the "Second Louisiana Purchase" was coined by Westbrook Pegler to identify the end of federal indictments and the corruption that ensued.

Even though Leche continued to expand the social programs of Long, his interests were more personal than public. Long had been a vocal critic of big business, and the biggest business he could attack in Louisiana was oil. Standard Oil made a good target. The criticism stopped with the election of Leche. Leche also put into place a regressive sales tax. This was in total conflict with the Long principles. He also gave tax exemptions to new businesses and industries, which were principles that Huey deplored. This included a ten-year property tax exclusion. Leche also supported and had passed a 1 percent sales tax that he signed into law.

The Roosevelt administration not only sidestepped the tax evasion charges against the Louisiana administration but it also started the flow of federal funds to the state. While individuals in Louisiana only received fines of a thousand dollars, others would have normally netted years in prison. Louisiana State University began receiving its share of funds, as did the Leon Weiss—designed New Orleans Charity Hospital. These funds didn't only help the needs of the public but also helped line the pockets of the Leche administration. Leche took the Roosevelt hands-off approach to Louisiana as a sign that he would be given a free rein to pillage the coffers of the government and the pockets of the businesses whenever the opportunity arose. The second Louisiana Purchase was under way.

While Leche was strengthening his hold on Louisiana, Fields was building his federal team in Shreveport. The offices of the federal attorney for the Western Region of Louisiana was located in that center of the North Louisiana oil fields. Fields moved into an apartment in Shreveport but refused to officially move from his beloved Farmerville. While Fields was setting up office in Shreveport, Leche was moving into his new residence at the governor's mansion in Baton Rouge. Both had strong roots that can be traced to Huey Long, both knew each other. Both started 1936 in a new role, and both had bright futures, but neither knew that they were on a collision course that would end in judicial combat in the courtrooms of Central Louisiana.

Although the perception may be that the Leche administration was doing nothing but lining their own pockets, the state was experiencing a certain amount of growth from funds that had a base in federal programs. A certain amount of internal state development was under way. Bridges, hospitals, and infrastructure projects were carried out from the 1936 to 1940 period. A state mineral board was developed, as was a department of commerce and industry. Also, a state conservation bill was enacted. This and the ten-year tax exemption for new businesses were progressive in nature while at the same time attracting factions that were in conflict with the Long doctrines. The Roosevelt administration must have found relief in the direction that Louisiana politics was going. Standard Oil was now an ally to a state's administration that had previously aggressively attacked it. Long was gone, and the state administration was doing everything to appease Washington.

In June of 1936, Franklin Roosevelt made a trip to Texas. During the trip, he took the opportunity to meet Sam Houston's ninety-year-old son, laid a wreath at the Alamo Chapel, spoke in Austin, and ultimately ended up at the Cotton Bowl in Dallas. While in Dallas, Roosevelt would meet with Leche. The Louisiana legislature was in session when Roosevelt was in Texas. Leche played the political game well and ordered the Louisiana legislature to adjourn and reconvened it in Texas.

While Roosevelt was giving his San Jacinto speech, his secretary, Steve Early, quietly informed him that Alfred Landon would be selected by the Republicans to run against him. This provided an opportunity for Leche to make additional political gains with this announcement. Dick had the Louisiana delegation pass a resolution while in Texas that praised God for providing "a great leader, Franklin Delano Roosevelt, who saved the nation from ruin and chaos." He then sent a message to the Republican Party during the speech that they should withdraw Landon from the race and allow Roosevelt to go in unopposed. The LSU band then burst into a rendition of Huey Long's "Every Man a King." It is unlikely that Roosevelt had ever witnessed such an impromptu show directed at him. Leche had earlier built a bridge to Roosevelt, which he now continued to strengthen. It's certain that Roosevelt had a clear understanding of the support that was now coming from Louisiana. He no longer had to worry about ghosts from the Long administration.

In May of 1937, Roosevelt made a swing to the Deep South by rail. The tour stopped at Biloxi, Mississippi, where he was escorted by Mississippi's Senator Pat Harrison and Governor Hugh White to the Jefferson Davis estate. At the time of the visit, the estate had been turned into a home for Confederate veterans. After the tour of the historical site, the entourage traveled to the home of Senator Harrison in Gulf Port. Waiting for the president's arrival was his son Elliott and Governor Leche.

The convoy boarded its train and left the quiet and beautiful oceanfront town of Gulf Port and headed west to the metropolis of old-world charm that was vibrant with new-world commerce and politics. On April 27, 1937, President Roosevelt had arrived in New Orleans. Waiting to greet the train was New Orleans mayor Sidney Maestri. Under the Long administration, Maestri was the commissioner of commerce. Now he was graciously welcoming the biggest opponent in Long's career. Also on the train platform was Seymour Weiss, another Long insider.

The May 10, 1937, an issue of *Time* magazine carried the following excerpt about the visit of Roosevelt to New Orleans.

> These three Longsters had every reason to return the Presidents cordiality, for the Long State machine and the Farley National machine are now on terms of mutual respect and cooperation. The Louisiana prohibition against New Deal money has been abolished, and WPA millions now flow freely into Louisiana. The old income tax indictments, including that of Mr. Weiss, have been quashed.

Two years earlier, the city would be screaming the ideals of Long's Share the Wealth, but this was changing. Quiet were the rants that opposed the Roosevelt New

Deal, as was Huey's laws that forbid spending relief money in Louisiana. Money was flowing into the state from the federal relief funds, and Roosevelt felt confident in his newly made ally in the state of Louisiana.

After the Roosevelt followers departed from the laurels provided by the Louisiana political moguls, the group went to the famous Antoine's restaurant. This world-renowned restaurant, which is located in the French Quarter of the city served the delegation its famous oysters Rockefeller and Pompano en papillate. Leche was present as should be expected of the head of the state government. Had Huey remained in power, it is doubtful that the Louisiana trip would have happened at all, and it is certain that if it had the accolades heaped on Roosevelt, it would have been suppressed, if not curtailed altogether.

The 1937 trip was not the first visit by Roosevelt to New Orleans. In 1928, Roosevelt made a sweep through the city. He was escorted by none other than Harvey G. Fields. Fields reminded James Farley of this visit in a letter he sent in 1934. In this letter, Fields sternly requested that Washington allow Louisiana to deal with its own internal politics and thus provide a "fair deal" in the political process. In other words, Louisiana would take care of its electorate and the feds can stay out of Louisiana politics. This also highlighted that Fields, although a major part of the Long political machine, would cross the political line to do what he felt was right.

Very few people would protest a decision made by the head of the National Democratic Party and the president of the United States. Fields wasn't the typical political creature, and if he felt something wasn't fair, or if a law was in question, he would quickly voice his position. This demonstrates a position of self-confidence manifested from the realization that if the right thing is done, an individual is ultimately rewarded for his good deeds. Fields was more interested in the good that could be achieved by a position rather than the power that was provided from the position. This came in part from his study of Theodore Roosevelt and the communication he had with this charismatic leader. Also, his use of the term "fair deal" is classic TR.

This letter to Farley follows.

LOUISIANA PUBLIC SERVICE COMMISSION

HARVEY G. FIELDS, CHAIRMAN
  FARMERVILLE, LA.

WADE O. MARTIN,
  ST. MARTINVILLE, LA.

FRANCIS WILLIAMS,
  NEW ORLEANS, LA.

BATON ROUGE

P. A. FRYE, SECRETARY
  BATON ROUGE, LA.

ALEX GROUCHY,
  ASST. SECTY. AND GEN. FIELD AGENT

IN REPLY PLEASE REFER
TO OUR FILE NO.

Farmerville, Louisiana,
August 31st, 1934.

Honorable James A. Farley, Chairman,
National Democratic Committee,
Washington D.C.

My dear Mr. Farley:-

                    We are in the midst of one of the
hottest and most severe political battles over the nomination for Congressman of the Fifth District of Louisiana that
has ever been known in the history of this State since the
primary law of 1906.

                    It has been rumored that influences
from Washington would be exerted in favor of Honorable Riley
J. Wilson, the present Congressman, who has four good true
and tried democrats, distinguished gentlemen, opposing him
for that office.

                    As Chairman of the Democratic Committee
of this District and of my County and as a Member of the State
Democratic Central Committee, and independent, belonging to
no faction and one of the original Roosevelt democrats and
organizers of his Clubs in this State, all I want to see is
a square deal for all of the candidates.

                    Although I am a friend and admirer of the
President, strong as I ever was for him, I cannot support
Riley Wilson, but I am willing to accord to him a fair deal
as head of the party in this District, so I am writing to
ask as Head of the Party Organization that no influence or
assistance come from any of our National Leaders to him or
anyone else in this campaign in the Fifth District, as we
are all good Roosevelt Democrats and should be allowed to
fight our battles out without any interference whatsoever.

LOUISIANA PUBLIC SERVICE COMMISSION

HARVEY G. FIELDS, CHAIRMAN
FARMERVILLE, LA.

WADE O. MARTIN,
ST. MARTINVILLE, LA.

FRANCIS WILLIAMS,
NEW ORLEANS, LA.

BATON ROUGE

P. A. FRYE, SECRETARY
BATON ROUGE, LA.

ALEX GROUCHY,
ASST. SECTY. AND GEN. FIELD AGENT

IN REPLY PLEASE REFER
TO OUR FILE NO.

#2-----JAF.

made. I, as one, who took the President over the City of
New Orleans, when Chairman of the State organization, who
organized his first clubs, who admires this peerless leader
and has an abiding faith in his wonderful qualifications and
in his sincerity deplore the fact that a few small bore politicians are hampering our cause in Louisiana.

Soliciting your splendid capacity and energy
in behalf of a fair deal in this District, which I feel sure
you are for, and with kindest regards and best wishes, I am,

Sincerely yours,

Harvey G. Fields.

HGF/m.

It's interesting to note that the man identified in the letter, Riley Wilson, was not new to Louisiana politics. At the time of Field's letter to Farley, Wilson was the standing U.S. Representative representing the Fifth Congressional District. He had also been a candidate for governor in 1928 but was defeated by Huey P. Long. It's unclear if Long was directly involved in the action to get Wilson out of office, or whether the letter was simply a notice to Washington to keep away from Louisiana politics.

Fields had written Riley Wilson in 1933 when he went to Washington to discuss building a set of locks and dams on Bayou D'Arbonne. D'Arbonne is a bayou in Union Parish near Farmerville. The D'Arbonne meanders through the parish and empties into the Ouachita Rive near Monroe. The construction of locks on the bayou would have made the waterway navigable to transport produce, and thus greatly enhance the commerce of Farmerville and the rural area around it. This work was never approved by the federal government. It wasn't until the early 1950s that Harvey's son, Thomas T. Sr., introduced a bill into the Louisiana House of Representatives to have a dam built across the D'Arbonne for the purpose of developing a major recreational lake. The bill unanimously passed in the House of Representatives. The day the bill was presented for signature by the chief executive, it was immediately signed into law by Governor Earl K. Long. This lake is now a major financial boom for the area.

The letter to Wilson follows.

September 18th, 1923.

Honorable Riley J. Wilson,
227 House Office Building,
Washington, D. C.

Dear Sir:-

    I will leave here Wednesday afternoon, the 20th, for Washington, probably driving at least half of the way, so that I should be in Washington Friday and Mr. Miller and Bro. Roberts will come on in the car, meeting me there Friday night or Saturday morning.

    I am enclosing a copy of application which will be presented by me to the War Department, pertaining to dredging the Bayou D'Arbonne, also asking for locks and dams, which I will be glad to have you join me in presenting as it is located in your district, and I am assuming you will be glad to help present the matter.

    It has been the subject of discussion here for over twelve months and twice acted upon by the Lions Club, but never has yet been presented before the proper Department at Washington.

    With kindest regards, I am

                Yours very truly,

HGF/hmm....

Fields had little to do with the Leche administration. For a man who had been a beacon for the common man, Fields was surely bothered by what he was witnessing in the politics of the state. Huey had, on occasion, used unscrupulous means to achieve his policies; however, these policies were directed at helping the oppressed. Huey loved the attention he received, as well as the display of power, by getting the results he desired. Leche also used unscrupulous means, but his love for the populace took a backseat to his administration's desire to enhance their personal wealth.

During the Leche term, Fields also had very little, if any, correspondence with Earl Long. Although previously a member of the same law firm, and as both men were active within the Huey Long administration, there was no alliance between the two. Earl was not handpicked by Huey to be a successor but did receive the nod for the number two position. Fields always felt that Huey was the brains behind the law firm and the party.

Earl was playing the political card well. The policies that had been the hallmark of his brother's administration were being scrapped while he was serving the state as the lieutenant governor. He kept a low profile while the administration in power was violating the trust of the electorate. Unlike Fields who would be outspoken when an injustice was happening, Earl bided his time and waited for an opportunity to present itself that would allow him to achieve his goal. Unknown to Earl, Fields was going to help provide this opportunity.

The Leche administration contained several key individuals that were major players in the Long organization. In addition to Earl who had been picked by the Long organization to be Leche's lieutenant governor, Seymour Weiss became a close confidant of Leche's.

Weiss was a self-made success. In 1923, he became the manager of the barbershop in the New Orleans Grunewald Hotel. That same year, the hotel's name was changed to the Roosevelt in honor of former president Theodore Roosevelt. The year after he became manager of the barbershop, Weiss was named the hotel's assistant manager. He was so successful with his management skills that Weiss was named the hotel manager in 1928. In 1931, he became president of the New Orleans Roosevelt Corporation.

Weiss was associated with a hotel that was very creative in its ability to produce the ambiance that attracted customers. The hotel had a nightclub in its basement that was touted as being the first nightclub in America. In the 1920s, this nightclub made quite an impact to the visitors of New Orleans. With its manufactured stalactites and indoor waterfall, the establishment was appropriately named the Cave. Patrons would enjoy the chorus girls while listening to New Orleans Dixieland jazz.

Weiss was extremely gifted with his managerial abilities, as well as with his ability to provide support to the politician that allowed him the opportunity for power and wealth. He was not a politician himself, but he was the man in the background that developed the machine and kept it running. In 1928, when Fields was working closely with Huey, Weiss became an insider of the Long administration. Long made the Roosevelt the campaign headquarters for his gubernatorial race. Long later used the Roosevelt to support O. K. Allen's run for the governorship. It was also in the middle of the night that Leche was summoned to the Roosevelt to be offered the secretary position for Allen if elected.

During the Long years, Leche was president of the Louisiana Democratic Association and the Huey Long secret political fund. This demonstrates the confidence placed in Weiss by Huey. During the depression, Weiss controlled the federal relief funds for Louisiana. He was also vice president of the Long-structured Win or Lose Oil Company. After Huey was shot, Weiss was at his bedside. Following his death, Weiss was made the chairman of the Huey P. Long Memorial Commission. Several years later, following the prosecution of Leche, Harvey G. Fields took over this position.

When Leche was tapped to inherit the power in the state, Weiss jumped on the Leche train, as had numerous other Long supporters. He became a leading member of the administration. Unfortunately for Weiss, he fell in line with the nod-and-wink assumption that Louisiana was now hands-off by the feds and funds were ripe for the picking. He joined Leche when indictments were eventually handed out.

During the Long administration, Huey had started a paper, *American Progress*, to spread his idealistic vision. So controversial was the paper that he had to have it printed in Mississippi. Leche understood the power of the pen and continued the *Progress*, which remained a statewide distribution. At a $2-a-year subscription rate, it was expected that state employees would subscribe while companies with state contracts were expected to advertise. Leche spent $200,000 to have a new printing plant built in Hammond, Louisiana. Leche was continuing his growth and solidifying his power within the state and the federal government.

The adage "Three's the charm" is no more true than what happened with the Leche administration in 1939. Prior to Roosevelt taking office, Hoover's administration was building its case against Huey Long and his organization. Roosevelt had that investigation halted. It wasn't long after Huey took office that he began his attacks on the Roosevelt administration. A second investigation began but was soft-soaped following the death of Huey and the pledge of loyalty by Richard Leche. Dubbed the Louisiana Purchase for the trivial fines imposed on members of the administration, this action was seen as a way for Roosevelt to gain Louisiana as a staunch ally. Eventually, the cost became too great.

A blind eye can only be turned as long as there is no challenge from someone that brings a wrong to light. Eventually, there was too much negative dialogue coming from Louisiana. In our present-day age of information, it's hard to fathom how such corrupt happenings could take place for so long. In the 1930s, there was no television. Radio broadcasting was the best way to get to the major populace. Newspapers were not universally distributed as they are today, and in many cases, politicians owned and distributed their own papers.

In February 1939, Fields wrote to Farley and requested a private meeting. Fields was so concerned about the communiqué's confidentiality that he asked that a response be sent to his private residence in Farmerville instead of to his federal offices in Shreveport Farley. It was not available when Fields was in Washington, but Fields did leave a package with his private secretary. Fields wrote to Farley to explain his actions. There is no record of what the package contained; however, the investigation of Leche began soon afterward. It's also important to note that information pertaining to high-profile politicians could have been easily discounted if provided by an individual from the private sector of society. It is hard to ignore when this information is presented by a United States district attorney.

Farmerville, Louisiana,
February 8, 1939.

Honorable James A. Farley,
Washington D.C.

Dear Mr. Farley:-

I am planning on being in Washington
Tuesday or Wednesday, and there is a matter I would
like to talk to you about, which will only take fifteen
or twenty minutes, not more than thirty minutes, but
I can crowd it into less time if you are busy on any one
of the days I am there, what I am writing to know is
whether I could see you either on Tuesday or Wednesday,
and would appreciate a reply as to what day, hour and
time would be convenient.

The matter I desire to talk to you about
is one I do not care to write about. Way back yonder,
before the President was elected, you will remember I
gave you and he certain information that proved to be
an advantage, and there are some things that I care to
discuss which I think you should know.

Upon receipt of this letter if you will
address a reply to Farmerville I will get it in time, as
I expect to leave my Shreveport office and spend Saturday
night and Sunday here, and would much prefer that the
reply to this letter be mailed to Farmerville instead of
my office at Shreveport.

Hoping that I can have the pleasure of
seeing you, and with kindest regards, I am,

Yours sincerely,

Harvey C. Fields.

hgf/m.

Farmerville, Louisiana,
February 23, 1939.

Honorable James A. Farley,
Washington D.C.

Dear Mr. Farley:-

      I went by your office the other after-
noon, had the pleasure of meeting Miss Corn, finding
out that she was your confidential Secretary, I took
the liberty of leaving an extremely personal and private
message which I hope you received on your return, which
I think contained facts well worth coming within your
knowledge, and that I would not have given except to one
that I knew was a friend who would treat the same as
confidential.

      Hoping that you received the message,
and remaining ready to be at your disposal at any time
you need me, I am,

          Yours sincerely,

          Harvey G. Fields.

HGF/mm.

One week after Fields sent the first letter to Farley, he left for Washington. The
date was February 12. The official purpose of the trip was to request additional
resources and a special assistant to help with fraud and insurance. The reason for
the request, to investigate fraud associated with WPA projects. Fields was building
a case against corruption in Louisiana. A copy of the press release associated with
the trip follows.

FIELDS LEAVES FOR WASHINGTON D.C.

Harvey G. fields, United States Attorney, left Shreveport via Illinois Central last night for Washington, D.C., where he will spend the next few days in conference and on official matters, then leaving for a couple of days visit to New York City on personal matters.

It is understood that Mr. Fields will discuss with officials and representatives of the Department of Justice a request for additional assistance and for a special assistant in insurance and fraud cases now pending for the court, and while Mr. fields will not divulge any details it is understood that reports from four parishes charging irregularities and alleged fraud connected with several WPA projects will be the subject of discussion, but the only comment made by Fields was:

"It is true that several reports have been made by a committee of citizens from three parishes that irregularities have been committed on some of the public projects but as to whether these reports are well founded is absolutely unknown to be and will become the subject of conference, probably resulting in an investigation on the part of the personnel department of the organization in control of the project."

The Police Jury of one of the North Louisiana Parishes this week adopted a resolution condemning the policies of the welfare office and project directors in their parishes, and committees from Jackson, Webster and Union are said to have waited on the United States Attorney this week with eh results that inspectors and personnel agents were in conference for several hours at Farmerville with Mr. Fields on Saturday afternoon, but the results of the conference and the nature of the reports made has not been disclosed. A full decision as to what course will be pursued will follow after the visit of the United States attorney to Washington.

Mr. Fields did state: "I have found to my surprise that the Government agencies have nothing to do with assignments in the beginning, and that if anyone is put on the WPA roll, or relief rolls, that did not merit going on, or anyone was kept off that should have been put on, that the first placing of persons and eligible is by the Public Welfare Committee on the various parishes and that in some instances where there are irregularities in the public welfare office we have no jurisdiction whatsoever, and they are managed through a state director."

"Now if a timekeeper, foreman or Police Juror causes any of the funds to be used on the projects improperly then there is a federal violation."

"The WPA and PWA organizations have very little to do with the selection of the parties when they are first taken. They take the list as given them by the parish committee, but thereafter if reports are made to them they will check up for discrepancies and irregularities and the committees

from several parishes have appeared asking for our opinion and to know
what constituted violations of the law, and in one instance resulting in a
petition being transmitted to my department asking for information as to
what the jurisdiction of this office was the matter."

Under the resolution just passed before the Senate and House in
Washington a check up of the situation will be made, as we understand the
law, and our interpretation of that statute is that from now on it is against
the law for any director, time keeper, supervisor, foreman or officers in
charge of relief work on Government project to interfere with, influence
or try to change the position or vote of any worker in any election of any
kind, to change the worker, employee or laborer in his views on any public
or political issues, and against the law for refund or donation to be made
back from the laborer or employee to his superior officer in charge or
directing the project upon which said employee, laborer or employees
are engaged.

Fields must have been in a dilemma during the last part of the 1930s. He
reported to the attorney general of the United States. When he came into office,
the attorney general was Homer Cummings. Then in 1939, when things were about
to bust loose in Louisiana, Cummings was replaced by William Murphy; and then
in the middle of everything, Murphy was replaced by Bob Jackson in 1940. Jackson
was replaced in 1941 when he was appointed by Roosevelt to the Supreme Court in
his attempt to pack the court with Roosevelt judges. Fields had to feel that he must
act independently on occasion as he prepared cases for the government. His chain
of command was going through too many changes to be highly efficient during this
important period of time.

June of 1939 was the point in time that the train officially started coming off the
tracks for the Leche political machine. Time Magazine reported in its' July 3rd edition
that Richard Leche had been named in federal charges pertaining to diversion of
WPA manpower and material for private uses in Louisiana. It was also noted that
there were serious irregularities in the LSU finances and its' president, James Smith,
had disappeared. The infamous "Louisiana Scandals" had begun.

James A. Noe of Monroe had formerly been made a floor leader of the Louisiana
Senate following a recommendation by Huey Long. He later became president
paro tempore of the state senate. Fate smiled on Noe while he was in office. When
Governor O.K. Allen died in office the lieutenant governor was next in line to assume
the governor position. At the time of Allen's death, Lieutenant Governor Forurnet
had all ready resigned to become a member of the Louisiana Supreme Court. This
left Noe next in line to take control of the state until the next election. During his
short time in office Noe appointed Huey Long's widow, Rose McConnell Long, to
complete Huey's vacated seat.

Noe and Fields were close friends. This friendship eclipsed the carnival atmosphere that surrounded Louisiana politics. Prior to becoming married, Noe's future wife taught Fields son in elementary school in Farmerville. Both Fields and Noe were devoted to Long and the causes he stood for. Even though they were loyal insiders of the Long administration, neither were indicted nor investigated during the tax evasion probe launched by the Roosevelt administration nor were they ever associated with the Lech administration.

Time Magazine reported in the same article of July 3rd that Washington columnists Drew Pearson and Robert Allen had been informed of the investigations by James A. Noe. Noe was hoping to better his chances of winning the 1940 gubernatorial elections by breaking the investigation to the press and stirring up the Washington news media. Noe did realize that he was probably going to have to go up against Huey's brother, Earl. Prior to Noe's notification to Pearson and Allen, the investigations had not hit the media nor had any press releases been provided. The investigation was at a point that it could have been quietly handled or even swept under the table as had happened in 1932.

Had Noe been he originator of the press notification or had he been coached? A pattern had developed pertaining to unidentified press releases and information that led to public knowledge of misconduct in office and flagrant breaking of laws. Who would understand this better than someone that had a good knowledge of the law, the power of the pen and the impact of the news paper on the populace. Fields himself could not directly notify the press and break the story as he was bound by his position and the tenants of his integrity to not do so. One thing is certain, once the story hit the press there was no turning back and the government had to move on with its' cases.

Leche had resigned office on June 22nd. He had been hospitalized for arthritis borne from bad teeth and this was the pretense for the resignation. The baton of power was passed to Earl Long, brother of Huey and a definite outsider of the Leche administration. *American Heritage* identified in it's August 1966 edition that Long had disliked Leche and was quoted as saying, "The office of lieutenant governor is a part-time job paying $200 a month. While I was lieutenant governor I spent twenty per cent of my time in Baton Rouge. The rest of my time I spent on a pea patch in Winnfield or practicing law n New Orleans." Long was never implicated in any of the scandals and it was noted that the Longs were always more interested in power than in money.

Attorney General Frank Murphy had sent to Louisiana the young Assistant Attorney General Otege John Rogge to investigate and prosecute. Rogge would be working with Fields to prepare the evidence and cases for the government.

By July 17th of 1939 Earl Long was quickly moving to make corrections in the state government. He ordered certain state officials to stop selling material to the state through companies they controlled. Long abolished the State Publicity Bureau which predominately consisted of contributors to the Leche Louisiana Progress and also announced that no one had to subscribe to or advertise in the *Louisiana Progress* to remain in good stead with the Governor.

Three days following Leche's resignation he announced a $500,000 shortage of LSU funds. Additionally, the president of LSU was missing. Earl had gone to work on this quickly by contacting WPA Administrator F.C. Harrington in Washington and requested any "data that you have obtained in a private way that would help us that has any bearing on the befuddled condition at LSU; also anything that you have found that has any bearing on irregularities involving an official or employee of the State of Louisiana." The LSU construction superintendent resigned and he, his assistant and a WPA foreman were arrested. They were charged with diverting WPA labor and materials for private use.

James Monroe Smith had hastily resigned as president of LSU just before he skipped town. He thought he would be safe in Canada but was quickly identified and returned by plane to New Orleans. A hoard of reporters awaited the now defunct president. One young reporter began asking pointed questions to Smith.

"I'll answer those questions later," Smith Snapped. "I don't know who you are but you are very impertinent."

"I thought you would remember me," the reporter responded. "You kicked me out of school four years ago."

Smith and his wife were quickly placed in a black police car and whisked away. With a lead car full of deputies and another loaded police car following Smiths car, two motorcycle policemen with sirens screaming lead the procession blasting through rural towns enroute to Baton Rouge at sixty miles an hour.

The Louisiana scandals were increasing at an accelerated pace by July 31st. A Federal Grand Jury had met and indicted Seymour Weiss. Immediately he resigned as the president of the main employment center in New Orleans, The Board of Docks. Weiss also resigned his position as the Commissioner of the New Orleans Police and Fire and President of the Port of New Orleans. It's also interesting that Weiss quietly paid the Internal Revenue Service in January, 1939 a total of $38,746.10 in back taxes and penalties for the years 1929-33. This was the same investigation that was originated by Hoover and Roosevelt had halted when he took office. Why he decided to make this payment is unclear but prior to this action Weiss had felt that he was beyond the laws that ruled society. After all, he had vowed undying loyalty to Roosevelt at the 1936 convention and then presented the president with twenty delegate votes.

By the end of July, LSU's defunct president, James Smith, had been indicted thirty-six times. Fourteen other men had also been indicted. Among them was an official of the Standard Oil of Louisiana, President of the Louisiana Medical Society and the Business Manager of LSU. Baton Rouge had fired its' police chief. Federal, State and Parish investigators were pouring over documents and investigating WPA and PWA irregularities, mail fraud, income tax evasion, LSU construction irregularities, "hot oil" law evasion, five percent deductions from state employees paychecks and anything else that could be uncovered. These were the exact issues identified in the Fields press release that caused him to travel to Washington and meet with the Department of Justice.

The Louisiana Scandals took the appearance of a shark frenzy. When blood is sensed from a wounded whale, sharks appear from everywhere and begin feeding in a frenzied attack. All that was required in Louisiana was for a few courageous men to say "enough is enough", asked that laws be enforced and justice be performed. Once the fuse was lit, it was just a matter of time before the explosion occurred and justice would be served. Political alliances had to be shed and replaced with the cloak of the laws of the land.

While the investigation was exploding through out Louisiana, Earl Long was preparing for the January elections. Jimmy Noe, who broke the investigations to the press before it was officially acknowledged by the government was evaluating his chances to be the next governor. Also watching the situation was reformist Sam Jones.

Weiss had been indicted as were other major and minor members of his state-wide organization. In August 14th it was announced in Time Magazine that Assistant Attorney General Rogge had indicted the man that Huey Long had nicknamed "Jughead". Former Governor Richard Leche would face a Federal Grand Jury on charges of defrauding the U.S Government by receiving a $67,000 cut from an illegal sale of state-owned oil land for $148,000. At the time he resigned the governorship and turned Louisiana over to Earl, he was quoted as saying when asked about what he was going to do, "I shall probably fool around some in the oil business."

When Leche's was indicted there was still one third of the leadership team associated with the administration that was untouched. New Orleans Mayor Robert Maestri was in power and his prestige was still in tact. Maestri enjoyed the power provided by both his office of Mayor of New Orleans and being one-third of the power base that inherited the Long organization. Where Maestri differed from Weiss and Leche was that he was satisfied with his elected position and didn't need to skim from the Federal coffers. He used his position to enhance his wealth but broke no Federal laws in doing so. Maestri was not indicted despite Federal Judge Thomas Davidson in Dallas stating that Maestri was just a guilty as Weiss and Leche in what was know as the "hot oil" case.

Huey's brother Earl took credit for much of Maestri's success. He stated, " You don't rewrite the Old Testament when you run for office. Look at Bob Maestri.If you're in politics, you want love. Man sold mattresses to the biggest bordello in New Orleans. He got elected mayor, his mattress sales shot up like a rocket. Bob was a shrewd man. I cultivated him after Hey died. Because a politician's first job: to make people feel good when they see you. Especially people who don't like you."

Long went on to say, " You can be a yellow-dog Democrat, and attack-dog Republican, a vegetarian poodle loyal to those Green people—but what every politician wants is love."

Leche and Weiss were both indicted on the "hot oil" scandal. This case was based on the sale of oil in excess of the states allowed maximum production levels. In this case it was income tax evasion that indicted the pair. Also indicted was Freeman Burford of Dallas. When Judge Davidson chastised the Louisiana Grand Jury for not indicting Mastri, he also refused to turn over Burford to Federal authorities in Louisiana.

Justice moved swiftly. Today, the time to prosecute a major crime that would be comparable to the Louisiana Scandals could take years. On September 15th of 1939 Seymour Weiss was found guilty of using the U.S. Mail to defraud the government. He was fined $2,000 and sentenced to thirty months in Federal prison. Also convicted with Weiss was former LSU president James Smith, his wife's nephew John Emory Adams and Lois LeSage, a suspended executive with Standard Oil of Louisiana. Their final guilt was based on selling $75,000 worth of furnishings to LSU from a Hotel that had all ready been sold to the university. While the actual fraud was a state violation not prosecutable by the Federal Government, the use of mail as a method to assist with the violation can be prosecuted by the feds. This is what the case was based on.

Smith spent two months in prison and returned to Baton Rouge to face the other charges against him. He plead guilty to four of the charges with a plea agreement where the remainder of the Federal and state charges were dropped. Following an unsuccessful suicide attempt Smith was sent to Louisiana's Angola penitentiary to serve his sentence.

In December Federal Attorneys began the prosecution of Abe Shusman, past president of the Levee Board and Bob Newman and Trent Harris, Jr, both prominent New Orleans Brokers.

By the end of February, 1940, the Leche organization which began as the Huey Long political machine ceased to exist. Over 200 people had been indicted by U.S and parish grand juries. Three had killed themselves, five pleaded guilty and five had been found guilty. The biggest plumb was picked when ex-governor Leche was convicted in Federal Court.

Charges against Leche consisted of using the mail to defraud, use of WPA funds to build his home and homes of allies, making a profit from "hot oil" and the misuse of funds intended for Louisiana State University.

Huey's prophesy was proven to be correct. He is reported to have said, "If these fellows ever try to use the power I've given them without me to hold them down; they'll all land in the penitentiary."

Jimmy Noe did run for governor as did Earl Long. Prior to the elections there were allegations of income tax evasion but Noe was eventually proven to be totally innocent. This smacked of political manicuring, Noe did not make the run off and Earl was pitted against reformist Sam Jones. Earl pleaded to the state voters that even one of Jesus's disciples was a "son-of-a-gun" and the Long administrations had a couple of bad apples as well. Don't judge himself because of what the Leche administration had done. The plea didn't work and in the Spring of 1940 Sam Jones, a reformist, became the next governor of Louisiana.

Following the prosecutions, Fields was up for re-appointment. Letters from scores of lawyers and the Louisiana Bar Association sent to the Attorney General and President Roosevelt embellishing Fields fairness and integrity plus numerous letters from members of congress requesting that he be returned to his position of Federal Attorney fell on deaf ears. Roosevelt had lost a clear ally in Louisiana when Leche resigned and a state that was a sure twenty delegates at convention time was now a toss up. There were other casualties for Roosevelt's support during this period of time. James Farley, the key to Roosevelt's success and good friend of Fields left the administration in disgust over various New Deal policies and Roosevelt's decision to run for a third term. Roosevelt had also broken with Al Smith, the man that Roosevelt had so vehemently supported for President in 1928. By the end of the war Roosevelt had likewise all but neglected his Secretary of State Hull and had cast him aside.

In the early days of 1941, Attorney General Jackson was not in a position to rock the Roosevelt boat as he had been hand picked to become the next Supreme Court Justice. Just as his predecessor, Murphy, Roosevelt was trying to stack the Supreme Court with his appointed judges. Jackson was noncommittal of the appointment of Fields.

A friend of Fields was Tom Clarke. He became an Attorney General in the early 1940s and was later placed on the Supreme Court by Harry Truman. He would have been the head of the Justice Department that Fields would have worked for if he had received another appointment. Ironically, in 1946 Clarke, in his capacity as Attorney General of the U.S., fired John Rogge, the assistant attorney general assigned to the Louisiana Scandals. He was terminated for identifying in a speech secret information pertaining to Nazi Europe. This ended Rogge's public life. Tom Clarke proved his integrity when in 1968 he resigned as a Justice of the Supreme Court when his son, Ramsey, became the Attorney General of the United States under President Nixon.

In 1945 Leche was up for parole. Fields went to Washington at his own expense to plead for Leche's parole. When he was queried why he had done this, Fields explained that by successfully prosecuting Leche he had done his job. Leche had served his time, had been a good prisoner and now deserved to be released.

Leche was released on parole following the meeting of the parole board. In 1953 he was pardoned by Harry Truman. When Harvey died Richard Leche called Fields' son and offered his condolences. He also related that he held no ill feelings for Fields and felt that he was a man of honor and integrity.

In 1941 the Louisiana Scandals were over. Roosevelt had lost a sure thing in Louisiana delegates; however, his health was beginning to fail and it was uncertain if he would ever be a viable candidate again. Jackson was on the Supreme Court, the prisons held many a son of Louisiana and the winds of war were beginning to blow harder; thus attention was shifted away from Louisiana.

Fields wrote in January 1941 to a son serving in the navy and confided that it looked like he would not be returned to his post. He noted that Earl Long and Senator Allen Ellender would probably not support his bid so he was preparing for his next step in life. Fields also related to his son that war would be starting very soon, possibly as early as April and it would most likely begin in the Pacific around the Philippines.

As catastrophic as the Louisiana Scandals were to the Leche administration supporters, the biggest loser was Huey Long. Much of the purely selfish and criminal actions performed between 1936 and 1940 were later associated to Huey. Thus was Huey's legacy provided by his hand picked cronies.

Fields made reference in several letters to the scandals and his part in the prosecution. In 1941 Fields wrote to newly elected Governor Sam Jones. At that time Hot Springs, Arkansas was noted for its' hot spring healing powers. People from around the country would travel their to relax and heal. Jones went to Hot Springs following the rigors of the 1941 elections. That is where field sent a letter requesting support on his re-appointment and also referencing his work with the Louisiana Scandals. This letter follows:

Farmerville, Louisiana.
January 8th, 1941.

Governor Sam H. Jones,
Hot Springs, Arkansas.

Dear Governor:

        I am sorry to see in the press that you are sick and having to recuperate up there, but after all when a man goes through a strain you have gone through it is better to take a complete rest.

        I went through fire and brimstone during the last public scandal investigation, but fortunately my greatest assets has been vitality and good health, so I managed to escape.

        I hope you are recuperating and that you will soon be back to your desk.

        I hesitate to write you, because of the fact that you are there for a rest, but inasmuch as the question of my re-appointment comes up in a few weeks, I am writing to say that I will appreciate any good word or approval statement you could make to any of the delegation or to the Attorney General of the United States.

        I feel that a good word from you will go a long ways. I understand up to date no other name has been filed and a great many members of the bar all over Louisiana have written the Attorney General in my behalf.

        With kindest wishes for your permanent recovery, and thanking you for anything done in my behalf, I am

        Yours sincerely,

        Harvey G. Fields
        U. S.District Attorney
        Western District of Louisiana.

Fields also solicited support for his reappointment from Attorney B. M. Dorrity. Fields noted in the letter that he had been the state district attorney from 1922 to 1926, had prosecuted over a thousand cases, and had a conviction rate of 97 percent. This was unprecedented. Fields also referenced that every jury seated by him during the Louisiana scandals convicted the defendant. The most extraordinary metric Fields noted was that in his four years as federal district attorney, he never lost a case. It was also noted that he had successfully managed the campaign for Senator Overton, who was one of the two senators that would determine his fate. This letter follows:

Farmerville, Louisiana.
January 8th, 1941.

Mr. B. M. Dorrity
Wilkinson Street,
Shreveport, Louisiana.

Dear Sir & Friend:

Your letter received and beg to say I was indeed glad to hear from you and of course your letter made me happy. Making Mrs.Fields even happier. I can never forget your loyal friendship to me in my political battles and in other battles, and I want you to know that I will always be ready to reciprocate. We all feel like you are a part of our family.

I am going to impose on you once more. I wish you would write Congressman Brooks, Washington, D.C., that you understand my term and that of my staff will expire withinthe next few weeks and that you as a friend of his and a citizen of Louisiana endorse and approve the work done by our department, and that you hope I will be re-appointed by President Roosevelt. Do not let him know that I have asked you to write the letter.

Also write Honorable Robert H. Jackson, Washington, D. C. stating what you know about my work, that you approve it, and if you choose to make special mention of the fact that as a state prosecutor from 1922 to 1926 I prosecuted and convicted more than one thousand people of the Third Judicial District of Louisiana and made a record of ninety-seven percent.

You can also, if you choose, mention the fact that in the Louisiana scandals in every case where the jury was selected by me not a single defendant was acquitted, and my record as U. S. Attorney that I have never lost a case.

I wish you would have those two lawyers you are very close to write a letter. A large number of the Shreveport Bar have already endorsed me, four Congressmen have endorsed me, and the department wants me re-appointed, of course both senators have to vote. Senator Overton has always been my friend and I once managed his campaign for U. S.Senator, managing it successfully.

With kindest regards, and best wishes for a happy year, I am

Yours very truly,

The conviction rate referenced in the letter is amazing. Fields was driven to achieve perfection, and the true winners were the residents of Louisiana and the United States. Fields was comfortable, knowing he had done his job.

Fields received a letter from a prominent lawyer in New Orleans. The lawyer was not only congratulating Fields, but he also told Fields that when he was involved with his cases, he would recommend a plea instead of going to trial. This letter follows.

DALY & HAMLIN
LAW AND NOTARIAL OFFICES
712 MAISON BLANCHE BUILDING
NEW ORLEANS

BERNARD J. DALY
WALTER B. HAMLIN

December 3, 1940.

Hon. Harvey G. Fields,
Farmerville, Louisiana.

Dear Harvey:

      I received The Bernice News-Journal of November
29th, with your Armistice Day Speech therein, for which please
accept my thanks. You know, I am a believer in saving good
stuff, and I am cutting your speech out and putting it in my
scrap book for future reference in the event I am called upon
to make a patriotic address. I hope you will not mind or
throw anything at me if you happen to be in the audience.

      I notice that you and your staff have been convict-
ing them like trained pigs up your way. I congratulate you
on your success. I long ago realized the futility of fighting these cases and figured that the best way to handle the
entire thing was to do the best you can for your client by
way of a plea, unless, of course, the facts are such as will
justify a contest. I have seen very few cases where the facts
justify a contest. We happen to have one in our office at
the present in which it looks as though the demurrer is good,
but, outside of that, I don't have much hope.

      I know that you have been very busy, and that is
why I haven't written asking you to get in touch with us when
you come to New Orleans, but as soon as your work slacks up,
I hope that you will have time to have dinner with us when
you come to New Orleans again at one of our good old French
restaurants like we used to do. If possible, I hope that you
will be able to bring Mrs. Fields with you.

      With best wishes to you, Mrs. Fields, and the whole
family, I remain

                Sincerely yours,

                W. B. HAMLIN.

The Louisiana scandals were over, and Harvey Fields, a major contributor to
the downfall of the corrupt Louisiana administration, activist for the rights of the
American working man and advocate for equal treatment of every citizen, now only
had to wait to be reappointed to the position he had so valiantly served.

CHAPTER 7

REAPPOINTMENT

In 1939, Fields was living between his home in Farmerville and his U.S. district attorney offices in Shreveport. The U.S. government didn't have jurisdiction in certain state matters, and Fields, in his position of U.S. district attorney, could not prosecute violations of state law. Fields as a resident of Louisiana, just as any state resident, could act independently if he knew a law was being broken. He deplored corruption and would do whatever was necessary to ensure that the laws provided by the jurisdiction of the state would be enforced.

Shreveport is in Caddo Parish, and the Red River serves as the eastern border of the parish. Crossing the river places a person in Bossier Parish. Fields had heard of corruption in Bossier Parish, and the root cause was linked to the Mafia. Public officials were linked to the vice that was rumored as being rampant. Fields had heard enough, and he was going to see for himself if the stories were true. When he verified what he had heard was in fact true, he was in a dilemma. How could he get this wrong righted? Once again, he used the power of the press and the anonymous reporter to highlight misdoings and force civil servants that were sworn to serve the people that elected them to perform their job. A copy of the letter to the *Shreveport Journal,* the local newspaper, follows.

TO THE VOTERS AND LAW ABIDING CITIZENS OF BOSSIER PARISH.

Some time ago the writer's attention was called to the gambling and bootlegging in Bossier Parish. Not being aware of the true conditions I set out to find out for myself, and am passing on to you the conditions I found to be existing, and trust that when you have read this message you will do likewise.

First I found Joe Reno operating a gambling house on the Minden Road, about two miles from Bossier City, known as Blossom Heath. Here he has ROULENTTE, DICE, BLACKJACK, CHUCOLUCK, and any other gambling "JUST WHAT HAVE YOU". There is drinking rooms, yes a dance hall similar to the "OLD DIME A DANCE". Well to make a long story short this place makes anything I saw in Dear Old Mexico look calm.

In Bossier City proper I learned that the drug stores were serving soft drinks spiked with alcohol or a bottle of alcohol right over the counter. I stood around on the streets an hour or so and was disgusted with street drunks. Along about ten o'clock at night a lady could hardly walk the streets without passing a drunk.

Out on any road from Bossier City you can be supplied with any amount of whiskey you want. You can take your choice, drive up to the still and buy as much as you like or as little, and from the street bootleggers you can likewise be supplied.

Then I went out on the Coushatta Road where lo and behold, Joe Reno, not satisfied with operation of one hell hole had another. This monument to our fair parish is operated right at the entrance to the beautiful airport.

THINK IT OVER A GREASY DAGO, ACTING THE PART OF AL CAPONE, being constantly surrounded by his gunmen, running his gambling, bootlegging and cheap dance hall right in the eyes of the law abiding citizens. Some time ago sheriff Tom Hughes ran Joe Reno out of Caddo Parish for pulling a gangster parade in his parish. WHY SHOULD WE BE THE GOAT?

Now I ask you is the time not ripe for us to act? Why can't the district attorney see that something is wrong? What is George Huckaby doing that he will allow bootlegging to be so easy? Surely they are getting their part of the graft.

Mr. Padget's attention has been called to the conditions in Bossier Parish, and he has made the reply that he had visited these places and found them to be alright. Sure they are alright for Reno and Padget, and Reno running wide open gambling houses. Should it be alright for us to pay Padget to enforce the law and have such conditions as these? Now lets get busy and recall Padget and find an honest man for the place who will clean this parish up and make it a decent place to live.

The reason no name is signed to this, the gangster conditions in this parish is such a persons life is in danger who would try to expose the conditions. The gunman who attempted the life of officer Glenn under Joe Reno's orders and was convicted in Caddo Parish with charge of shooting with intent to murder officer Glenn, and got from eight to twelve years in prison is now in the employe of Joe Reno as one of his gunman. Such conditions keeps the writer from signing a name.

Few men would have had the courage to risk their lives in pursuit of justice, but few embrace the tenants of the Constitution and the laws of the country as aggressively as Harvey Fields.

Fields also made a courageous statement in 1939. He was a member of the Elks Club. He was also known to be a powerful speaker. His service as toastmaster and speaker at various functions was highly sought after. This ability served him well, and in 1939, he delivered a speech over radio station KWKH in Shreveport. This station was a flagship station for North Louisiana and East Texas and would later launch the careers of such immortals as Johnny Horton, Johnny Cash, and Elvis Presley. At a time that religion played a disproportionate part in the selection of elected officials; a time that racial equality was not a subject of discussion in most political circles, especially in the Deep South; and a time that the United States was witnessing the atrocities of war on far-off soil, Fields took a bold stand. This speech on Americanism and human rights follows.

ADDRESS OF HARVEY G. FIELDS ON AMERICANISM UN THE AUS-
PIECES OF THE NATIONAL BENEVOLENT PROTECTION ORDER
OF ELKS, OF SHREVEPORT, MARCH 1, 1039, RADIO
STATION KWKH

This is Harvey G. Fields of Shreveport speaking over station KWKH in behalf of the Benevolent Protective Order of Elks of Shreveport in line with the National Weekly Program on Americanism.

At this time in our history when we view other nations in distress and oppression of dictatorship, the threatening clouds of war, and men lined up by the thousands to destroy with cannon, airships, and destructive machinery of every kind, not only property and lives but the fundamentals upon which True Americanism was founded, how fitting it is that we should pause from our daily pursuits to defend Americanism, to remind our neighbors, our friends and our people of their duty to protect the principles upon which real Americanism rests, and to you should belong to the order of the Elks, a strictly American Order, remember that you above all others, because of the history of your order and the solemn oath that you take, with the American Flag flying over your head when you take the oath should be in the front ranks for tolerance and Americanism.

When Washington, Morris and Carroll, all of different faiths and creeds, signed the immortal, everlasting document which became the tenants of Americanism, they with inspired hearts and minds, planted as the most beautiful flowers in the garden of Independence, tolerance, justice, freedom, liberty and patriotism.

So let us, on this occasion, this week dedicated by the great order of the Elsk, and American institution which has unfurled over its crowned, exalted rulers, a half million members and their families, with the stars and the stripes as an emblem of charity, love, tolerance and friendship, bind ourselves as Americans to keep alive, watching out for hidden adversaries and enemies, those elements which will forever insure peace, happiness and tranquility to the American people and their future generations as intended by our forefathers when they founded this great republic.

Isms, false doctrines, and race or religious prejudices have no place in this country. All alike, the Jew, the gentile, the descendants of those from every land, who live in obedience to our laws, have equal rights and privileges. Let every man and good woman teach this ideal, love, tolerance and fairness to one another, practice these ideals, lover, tolerance and fairness in their relationship with one another and to one another in all instances and Americanism will live on.

In these tragic days when man's inhumanity makes countless millions mourn when racial and religious groups are oppressed elsewhere, persecuted by the ruthless damnable and barbarian practices of dictatorship, when the cherished ideals of democracy are being trampled upon, there is no greater moment of importance in America than to let every man, woman and child stand as a sentinel watching for an enemy, standing as a soldier to guard the immortal principles that we have inherited, and to remember there is one way to happiness. Love and peace can always be maintained, and teat is by upholding, protecting and maintaining democracy, religious freedom and tolerance, which all summed up together are Americanism.

To this great common altar of Americanism there comes daily into this country the Jew, the Protestant and the Catholic with the best traditions of each, coming to pray that their traditional rights may always be preserved, and the sacred altar of Americanism be preserved by an edict and the sanction of almighty god will not be blemished by the polluted and bandit hand of dictatorship or false propaganda spread among our people through those who would take from the heritage of the past and leave us with a false and cruel idol to steer us to anarchy and chaos in the future.

And why should no the Jew and protestant and the Catholic, together with the other various sects, come to this common altar in this great country or ours.

First and foremost it is fundamentally right. Second, we are a people who came from lands across the waters where oppression dominated at the time they came over. Third, and most important of all, highest and greatest of all the reasons we could set forth, do we not have the challenge of the old Bible? It is not true that after all is done and said that we have but one Father? Were we not created, after all is done and said, by one and the same God?

Civil and religious liberty with the rights and privileges given us under what is known in America as the Bill of Rights, a national jewel, adopted by all of the states of these United Commonwealths, stands as a gift not only from our forefathers, but from Almighty God, as they in turn were inspired by their Creator when they wrote the Declaration of Independence and the constitution of the United States, which guarantee freedom of thought, freedom of press, freedom of religion, and personal liberty as long as it does not interface with the rights of others, is not abused, and the laws of the country are obeyed and not entrenched upon.

To me it is necessary that the best of our people, old and young, should not forget the altar of Americanism, for when the day comes that that altar is forgotten, then America will cease to be a land of freedom.

At this common altar of Americanism let us steer the youth and the children of this historic land in order that in the days to come, when we have passed away to an unknown land, there will still remain an army and host of true Americans, plighted pledged to uphold the ideals, the noble sentiments, the achievements and the principles of real Americanism.

I thank you.

Fields felt that good was derived from the person and his beliefs and not from a political party that he belonged to. In 1932, Franklin Delano Roosevelt took office. At that time, the largest dam in the world was under construction near the small Nevada desert town of Las Vegas. Hoover Dam was well on its way to completion when the Democrats took power. The dam's name was then changed to Boulder Dam. Later the dam was rightfully given its original identity of Hoover Dam. However, Boulder City retained its name. Such was the dislike of the two political parties for each other.

Fields read an article written by Herbert Hoover in 1934. Fields was so impressed that he felt compelled to write to Hoover, commending him despite Fields's total devotion to the Democratic Party.

Farmerville, Louisiana.
September 11th, 1934.

Mr. Herbert Hoover,
Los Angeles, California.

Dear Sir:-

This will express my appreciation and
commendation of the article written by you and published
in the Post of September 8th, under the title of
"The Challenge to Liberty", and to say that while I
do not agree in every particular with your conclusions
or your recitals of fact that in the main you are correct.

Further in the first five paragraphs of the
article your discussion of freedom and liberty is a
one hundred percent jewel, brilliant because of its truth
and radiance, and further because the necessity of the
wearing of such a jewel by our officials of the nation
and of every state at this time.

It is decidedly the best article ever written
and published by you, better yet it will be productive
of considerable thought and action in this country
on the part of loyal Americans irrespective of party
affiliations.

Yours respectfully,

Harvey G. Fields, Chairman
Louisiana Public Service Commission.

HGF/hns....

Harvey Fields must have felt in 1940 that he was certainly in a position to retain his position as federal district attorney. He had performed admirably in both his assigned position and in his service to the Democratic Party. There was also another laurel he was to receive.

WHO'S WHO IN AMERICA LISTS
NORTH LOUISIANA CITIZEN.
- - - - - - - - - - - - - -

The publishers of Who's Who in America have included in their 21st biennial addition, now in course of preparation the name of Harvey G. Fields, United States Attorney.

Each two years the names of five or six prominent citizens in different walks of life in this State are listed as Americans entitled to be honored in the list of Who's Who in America.

The compilation will show his profession as a lawyer, that he as Federal Attorney is listed as having one of the highest percentages in America for convictions, that he is a descendant of William J. Fields, who was one of the five companions of Daniel Boone in his exploration of Kentucky, that he is a member of three lodges, one Greek Letter Fraternity, two National Clubs and has held nineteen public and party offices in his State, holds three degrees, and speaks three languages.

Three other selections will be made in Louisiana, which will include 1â is said the names of Mr. Fields, Governor Richard W. Leche and John H. Overton.

Mr. Fields, as Chairman of the Democratic Committee of the Fifth District came into the limelight pretty strong and successfully by up-holding the election laws and seeing that a fair count was gotten in the last election.

Most of people say openly yhat if it had not been for Fields active and able fight that frauds would have been allowed to parties, irregularities gone through with, and that Congressman Mills would not be sitting in the Ghair at Washington now.

Fields is a stickler for honest elections, he is fearless and knows the election/ laws of this State by heart and will do his duty as a party officer at all times, whether it meets the approval of any of his own crowd, or anybody else, stating openly that he believes the permanancy of democracy rests upon the right of the people to cast an intelligent vote, honestly counted and returned/

This was one of the three times that he was selected for this honor. Ironically, Richard Leche, the man that Fields helped to put in prison, was also selected as one of the three men to receive this award.

Fields was very proud of his accomplishments, and he did not want his name tarnished in any way. In 1939, someone had used his name in a newspaper story in the *Farmerville Gazette*. Harvey was furious and did everything but challenge the perpetrator to a duel.

FIELDS WRITES OPEN LETTER.

Shreveport, Louisiana,
March 7th, 1939.

Editor Farmerville Gazette,
Farmerville,
Louisiana.

Dear Sir:

It has come to my attention yesterday over the
telephone, by a message from a friend in Union Parish, that
someone had connected my name with an opposition movement
to the appointment of a successor to the late Pat Murphy,
Sheriff of Union Parish, which information came to me as a
shock and surprise, because of the fact that immediately
after the funeral services at Farmerville, I rushed to
Shreveport, accompanied by my Secretary, and entered upon
my duties here in the trial of a case before the Federal
Court, without any knowledge of what was happening over in
Union Parish.

I did not believe there was anyone in Union Parish,
who would stoop to such low and contemptible tactics as to
falsely link my name with any such transaction or movement,
particularly as I was a friend and neighbor of the late Sheriff,
had become exceedingly close to him in the last few years and
had stated to several parties that I hoped to see an appointment made, and to his widow, because it would avoid political
complications and besides be a most meritorious tribute to him,
so that no one was more pleased than I was when I heard over
the wire yesterday that the Governor had made such an appointment.

Because of the high position I hold, I am not able to
express my resentment in the language I would personally use
if I could face in person the degenerate falsifier who made
any such statement of misrepresentation, and in order that no
innocent person might unwittingly or unintentionally repeat the
said false statement, which suspicion points as being made by
a possible degenerate individual and politician, I respectfully
ask that your paper give proper publication to this letter.

Yours respectfully,

Harvey G. Fields.

Later, he was also misquoted in a statement pertaining to newly elected Louisiana governor Sam Jones. Again, he was infuriated and wrote to Governor Jones, explaining that he did not originate the statements.

Farmerville, Louisiana.
January 12th, 1941.

Governor Sam Jones
Baton Rouge, Louisiana.

Dear Governor Jones:

Your letter received and I thank you very much for your reply from Hot Springs.

I was in Little Rock yesterday on my way back from Nashville, where I have been representing the government for nearly a week in gasoline fraud cases, and my wife's sister-in-awl, who is a first cousil of the new governor, told us you would be at the inauguration. I was glad to find that you were going to be present. You will like Governor Atkins, because he is a plain,and honest gentleman, with practical ability, and was at one time a federal executive at Little Rock, having been United States Revenue Collector.

I am sending you a clipping that I found here on my return to Farmerville and in view of the fact that I see my name is boldly printed thereon, I am writing to say that this article is without any authority, consent or knowledge on my part, and that allthe the statements made therein are without any foundation, and I would not worry you with it, except and because of the fact that it leaves an inference that I do not want to exist, and I desire to say that at no time have I given any such information to the newspapers from which this article enimates, and that fully fifty percent of the statements made in this connection are erroneous, which I thought you should know as coming from me direct. I am assuming the same condition as to Viosca, but only speaking for myself.

I am glad to see in the paper to-day that you have fully recovered and will be at your desk again.

With kindest regards, I am

Yours respectfully,

Harvey G. Fields.

By the end of 1940, Fields was beginning to wonder why he had not heard from Washington pertaining to his reappointment. Roosevelt had been known to turn a blind eye on his loyal supporters when they were no longer in line with a new philosophy that he was developing. Roosevelt had lost contact with Al Smith, whom he had promoted for president. James Farley and Roosevelt were at odds, and Farley finally made a clean break with Roosevelt in 1940 when Roosevelt announced he would run for a third term, and thus remove any chances for Farley to be considered for the top post. Others were leaving the Roosevelt organization due to his attempts to expand the Supreme Court and pack it with Roosevelt Democrats. He would later exclude Cordell Hull, an extremely brilliant secretary of state from many cabinet meetings during World War II, and this action would eventually force Hull to leave the administration. By the end of 1940, Roosevelt's health was beginning to fail, and he was not the robust man that he was eight years earlier. In the early months of 1940, Roosevelt was on a cruise. Additionally, Bob Jackson, attorney general, was in line for a Supreme Court position.

Fields finally decided to force the subject, and he wrote to Robert Jackson, attorney general, and respectfully requested to be reappointed to his current position. This letter follows.

Farmerville, Louisiana.
January 8th, 1941.

Honorable Robert H. Jackson,
U. S. Attorney General,
Washington, D. C.

My Dear Mr. Attorney General:

I am reminded of the fact that my term as United States District Attorney will expire in the next few weeks, and I am taking this means to say that it has been a pleasure to be connected with the Department of Justice, as one of its attorneys.

If there is no objection and the department is satisfied with my work during my tenure of office I would be pleased to be re-appointed, and succeed myself, leaving that matter to your good judgment and our splendid leader and defender of the rights of the people, the President of the United States.

With kindest regards, and wishing you a happy year during 1941, I am

Yours sincerely,

Harvey G. Fields
U. S. District Attorney
Western District of Louisiana.

HGF/mm.....

MATTHEW F. McGUIRE
Assistant to the Attorney General

Department of Justice
Washington

January 17, 1941

Harvey G. Fields, Esquire
United States Attorney
Farmerville, Louisiana

My dear Mr. Fields:

The Attorney General has requested me to acknowledge the receipt of your letter of January 8, concerning your desire to be reappointed as United States Attorney for the Western District of Louisiana.

Please be advised that this matter is receiving the careful attention of the Attorney General, and you are assured that your request will have every consideration.

With kind regards,

Sincerely yours,

Matthew F. McGuire
The Assistant to the Attorney General

Fields solicited help for his reappointment from both legal and political sources. Many letters that extolled both Fields's professional qualifications and his professional and ethical character were provided. One letter was sent by a member of the Louisiana court of appeals and references the Louisiana Bar Association.

January 17, 1941.

Honorable Franklin D. Roosevelt,
President of the United States,
The White House,
Washington, D. C.

My dear Mr. President:

      I am taking the liberty of writing you with
reference to Honorable Harvey G. Fields, whose term of
office as United States Attorney in the Western District
of Louisiana will expire in the near future.

      I am personally well acquainted with Mr. Fields
and feel that he is eminently qualified in every way for
the office of United States Attorney and through my knowledge, as well as through general reputation, I believe
that he has proved this point by his services in the past.
In my opinion his reappointment is to the interest of the
State and Nation as well as a fitting reward for his past
services, and I, therefore enthusiastically endorse his
name for reappointment.

                           Respectfully yours,

PCR:ey

Fields was well respected by the legal profession in Louisiana. Numerous letters
were sent to both Robert Jackson and President Roosevelt on behalf of Fields.

Dec 31 1940

Hon Robert H Jackson,
Attorney General U.S,
Washington, D C
Deaprtment of Justice.

Dear Mr Jackson;

    Our present United States District At-
torney for the Western District of Louisiana, is an appli-
cant to succeed himself in that important office.

    In this District and State, the Bar re-
gards Hon Harvey G Fields as one of the most capable and
efficient and forceful prosecutors the Federal Department
of Justice has ever given us. Mr Fields is not only fair,
courteous,courageous and just,but he is firm and fearless
in the discharge of his official duties.

    Mr Fields is one of our most able and
successful lawyers and practitioners, and is a gentleman
of refinement and culture, whose high character is above
reproach. We should be disappointed if he were not selected
as his own successor, and we heartily and confidently com-
mend him to your favorable consideration.

    I hope you will permit me to express my
sincere best wishes for your continued successful administration of your high Department, and for the seasons
greetings.

       Yours very truly,

CVR ab

      Clem V Ratcliff,

Law Office

Robert J. Newson, Sr.

206 Ricou-Brewster Building

Shreveport, Louisiana

January 7, 1941

Hon. Robert Jackson
Attorney General of the United States
Washington, D. C.

Dear Mr. Jackson:

I understand that the Hon. Harvey Fields,
Federal District Attorney for the Western District of
Louisiana, is a candidate for reappointment, and I am
writing this unsolicited letter of reccommendation for
him, since I feel that he has proved himself to be a
fearless and impartial prosecutor. He was faced with
a difficult situation in office and did just exactly
as I did and felt that the State Administration, which
indorsed him, was no longer worthy of any consideration
after the evidence had pointed to their dishonesty and
he has conscientiously endeavored to do as a servant
of the people of the United States should do and mete
out impartial justice to everyone.

I have no axe to grind, since I have no
political aspirations and have never received one
penny out of politics; the only office I have ever
held being that of Democratic Committeeman. While I
have been high man for Louisiana in every Federal Civil
Service examination held for lawyers, I have never held
a Government position, except that of a Fee Attorney
when my services were needed and I have little, or no,
criminal practice for the very simple reason that I am
never able to get a reasonable retainer out of this
class of clients, but I do feel that Mr. Fields is trying to render all the people of the Western District
of this State the kind of service that he should, in
his present position, and I have never heard one word
of adverse criticism about him from anyone during his
term of office.

Copy

Sincerely yours,

Robert J. Newson

RJN:MF

OFFICE OF DISTRICT ATTORNEY
14TH JUDICIAL DISTRICT OF LOUISIANA
LAKE CHARLES, LA.

January 22, 1941.

Hon. Allen S. Ellender,
Senate Chamber,
Washington, D. C.

Dear Senator Ellender:-

    I understand that Mr. Harvey G. Fields' name will
be acted on within the next few days for reappointment.

    I have found Mr. Fields and his staff very courteous
and fair in the contact I have had with them. In matters that
I know of which the Grand Juries that he advised investigated
during the latter part of 1939 and the early part of 1940,
I think he acted fairly throughout. I know of several matters
in which radicals wanted Grand Juries in his District to take
action for political reasons, in which indictments were not
returned, and it is my belief that he and his staff went
thoroughly into the facts of the case.

    Some weeks ago various people made complaints that
the amendments were given more votes in the November 5th
election than they received, and Mr. Fields ordered the
ballot boxes impounded and investigated these complaints
immediately they were received by him.

    I personally should like to see him reappointed, as
I have found him fair in all matters in which I had any
interest.

    Wishing you Health and Prosperity during 1941, I
remain,

                    Yours sincerely,

                    C. V. Pattison
                    District Attorney

CVP/mmm
Blind Copy to: Hon. Harvey G. Fields,
              United States Attorney,
              Farmerville, Louisiana.

Fields received communication from newly elected governor Sam Jones. Jones noted that he knew of no other applicants for Fields's position. This surely gave Fields cause to feel optimistic about his chances for reappointment. Fields would have realized that under the Jones reformist administration, he would have been even more successful in clearing up the political corruption of Louisiana. Jones had gone into office as a reform candidate, and a major reason for this was Fields's aggressive prosecution of corrupt individuals and political bosses in the state.

STATE OF LOUISIANA
EXECUTIVE DEPARTMENT
BATON ROUGE

SAM H. JONES
GOVERNOR

Hot Springs, Ark.,
9 January, 1941.

Hon. Harvey G. Fields,
    Farmerville, Louisiana.

Dear Mr. Fields:

    Thanks very much for your letter of January 8. I
feel sure I will be out of the Hospital in a short time.

    I have heard of no other applicants for your po-
sition and will check into the entire matter when I go
to Washington, which will be in the near future.

                        Sincerely yours,

SHJ:dgl   Sam H. Jones.

Fields also received various letters from members of Congress pertaining to his reappointment.

A. LEONARD ALLEN
8TH DIST. LOUISIANA

HOME ADDRESS:
WINNFIELD, LOUISIANA

COMMITTEES:
FLOOD CONTROL
CENSUS
IMMIGRATION AND
NATURALIZATION
ELECTIONS NO. 1
WAR CLAIMS

D. M. RIDDLE, JR.
SECRETARY

Congress of the United States
House of Representatives
Washington, D. C.

January 17, 1941

Hon. Harvey G. Fields,
Farmerville,
Louisiana.

Dear Harvey:

     I have your letter of January 14th.

     In view of the fact that this is purely Senatorial patronage, I think the proper thing for me to do would be to discuss it with the two Senators. I shall avail myself of the first opportunity to do this. I am sure they will give your name most serious consideration. The Attorney General already has your record. It therefore seems to me to resolve itself into one question and that question confronts directly the two Senators.

     If you come up to Washington, drop in to see me. We are entering what will no doubt be a very critical year. We are down at hard work.

     With every good wish to you and the family, I am,

          Sincerely yours,

          Leonard Allen
          Member of Congress

ALA:c.

Fields's friend Newt Mills wrote to him to let him know that he had talked to one of the senators that would propose the reappointment, and it was looking favorable for Fields. Fields also received correspondence from Congressman Domengeaux.

NEWT V. MILLS
FIFTH DISTRICT LOUISIANA

COMMITTEES:
TERRITORIES
INSULAR AFFAIRS
PUBLIC BUILDINGS AND GROUNDS
WAR CLAIMS
CIVIL SERVICE

Congress of the United States
House of Representatives
Washington, D. C.

January 17, 1941.

Mr. Harvey G. Fields,
U. S. Federal District Attorney,
Farmerville, Louisiana.

Dear Mr. Fields:

The enclosure is self-explanatory; however, I have discussed your appointment with Senator Ellender and I am happy to state everything looks favorable.

With best wishes and kindest regards, I am

Your friend,

Newt V. Mills

Newt V. Mills, M.C.

NVM/cm
Encl.

Congress of the United States
House of Representatives
Washington, D. C.

January 6, 1941.

Hon. Harvey Fields
Federal District Attorney
Shreveport, Louisiana.

Dear Mr. Fields:

       It was a pleasure to comply with your request
in recommending your reappointment as District Attorney
of our district as evidenced by copy of letter which I am
enclosing to you and which I sent to the Honorable Robert
H. Jackson.

       I also discussed your reappointment with Congress-
man Plauche and he assured me that he would likewise recommend you for reappointment.

       From what I have been able to gather, I don't believe
that you will have any opposition, but should any develop and
you feel that I can be of further service to you, call upon
me without any hesitation.

       With all good wishes and regards, I am

                Very truly yours,

                JAMES DOMENGEAUX

JD:lb

The district attorney of Tallulah, Louisiana, received a letter from Roosevelt
pertaining to Fields.

THE WHITE HOUSE
WASHINGTON

January 21, 1941

My dear Mr. Snyder:

The President has received your
letter of January seventeenth, in which you
urge the reappointment of Honorable Harvey
G. Fields as United States Attorney for the
Western District of Louisiana. He appre-
ciates your courtesy in writing to him in the
interest of Mr. Fields, and asks me to bring
your communication to the attention of the
Attorney General.

Very sincerely yours,

STEPHEN EARLY
Secretary to the President

Jeff B. Snyder, Esq.,
District Attorney,
Tallulah,
Louisiana.

Despite the letters of encouragement from both members of Congress and Governor Jones, Fields had come to the reality that he would be replaced. Fields had turned politics upside down in Louisiana. He had sent to prison an administration devoutly loyal to Roosevelt, had taken on corrupt voting irregularities, and had prosecuted many elected officials. Fields was an uncomfortable thorn in the side of many officials regardless of how right and courageous he was in his role as federal district attorney. On January 30, Fields wrote to his son, Harvey Jr., and noted that it appeared that he would be replaced. Strangely, Fields noted that Earl Long was involved in the decision despite the fact that he had no direct involvement in the selection progress.

Farmerville, Louisiana.
January 30th, 1941.

C

O

P

Y

Mr. Harvey Fields Jr.
U. S. S. Corolla
c/o Postmaster
New York City, N. Y.

Dear Son:

        I am writing to tell you that Bob Kennon
dismissed and threw out your case last week before he
left for the army camp.

        I hope you are well and will be careful and
not make any mistakes and stand by the guns.

        Governor Jones and all of his congressmen endorsed
me for re-appointment, but I do not think Ellender and
Overton will do so and it is whispered around that someone
else will be replace me, and that Earl Long and the senators
have arranged not to endorse me, and of course the Department
will recommend who ever the senators endorse.

        Your mother has been sick, but is much better.

        Your wife has returned to Shreveport.

        With much love, I am

                     Yours devotedly,

                     Daddy

Fields was finally notified that his term would end on February 6. On February 22, he wrote to his son in Nevada and told him that his term had ended, but also noted that he was still performing his work as federal district attorney. He also noted that several politicians that had been pushing for his replacement were still going to be prosecuted. Fields refused to compromise his integrity, and he would work to the last day in carrying out the requirements of his job.

Farmerville, Louisiana.
February 22nd, 1941.

Mr. T. T.Fields
Wellington, Nevada.

Dear Son:

Your letter of the 8th received.

Since I wrote you Judge Rush Wimberly was convicted of contempt
of court for fooling with the jury, and I think Judge Dawkins
will give him six months or a year in jail. In the meantime
Mr.Standley got in touch with my office yesterday and I mailed
him copy of the proceedings, so I look for him to bring ouster
suit. The Wimberlys were among those who had wired the
senators many times to stop the prosecution, but it looks like
now they are going to answer for their sins and for their
violations of the law.

Jimmie Now is in the hospital at Hot Springs, has been there
two weeks and will be there a week or ten days longer.

Your mother got a letter from Harvey Jr. that he would probably
be given a discharge the 25th, but I wrote him to-day that
a military officer told me he would have to register within
five days and then he might be called out. I feel that we are
going to have some trouble with the far East section and have
felt so for many months ever since my trip to Washington in
November.

My term ended February 6th, and the plan was to have someone
appointed within a day or so and then confirmation by the 9th
or 10th, but up to date noone has been named, and it is possible
that I may finish my month out, and it will be in March before
my successor is named. In the meantime I am certifying a number
of matters to the State and making a report to the Attorney General
on several scandal cases advising him that they should be prosecuted
and that politicians were trying to interfer and stop the
prosecution, so that I will leave things in nice shape for my
successor and in such condition I am sure the cases will have
to be gone on with, and I can guarantee you that some of the
fellows who hoped to gain by my failure to be re-appointed will
have to face the music, some of them within the next few days,
as I have a term of court beginning at Shreveport Monday the
24th.

Fields actually remained in his position until May of 1941. Strangely, several locations on the Internet list Harvey Fields as being the federal district attorney of the Western District of Louisiana from 1937 to 1945.

Despite his disappointment, Fields still believed in the tenets of the founding fathers and continued his private practice and his support of the Democratic Party and worked for the poor and the oppressed.

The question still remains, what went wrong? It appeared that Allen Ellender was going to endorse him. Several congressmen stated this. Additionally, later correspondence from Ellender noted that they had remained friends up until the time of Fields's death. Overton, the other senator from Louisiana, was close to the Long administration, and Fields had helped manage his campaign. So where was the decision made to disavow Fields's reappointment?

In 1944, the Democratic National Convention was held in Chicago. Fields was not only a delegate, but he had been named a member of the Rules Committee. His keen knowledge of the workings of the convention that he had so successfully used in past conventions made him a perfect candidate for the position.

PROGRAM

American Democratic National Committee

PRE-CONVENTION CAUCUS

JUNE 19-20, 1944

HOTEL HAMILTON
CHICAGO · ILLINOIS

∞

OFFICERS

Chairman—GLEASON L. ARCHER
Boston, Massachusetts

Vice-Chairman—OTHA D. WEARIN
Hastings, Iowa

Secretary—ROBERT E. O'BRIAN
Des Moines, Iowa

Vice-Chairman—JOHN J. O'CONNOR
New York, New York

Treasurer—WILLIAM J. GOODWIN
New York, New York

Vice-Chairman—J. E. McDONALD
Austin, Texas

Assistant Treasurer—RALPH MOORE
Granger, Texas

Vice-Chairman—CHARLES H. McGLUE
Boston, Massachusetts

∞

HEADQUARTERS

Borland Building
105 South La Salle Street
CHICAGO · ILLINOIS

COMMITTEES

CREDENTIALS COMMITTEE
ROOM 403
JOHN REAGAN—Chairman
WILLIAM WARREN
J. E. McDONALD
LAWRENCE BURROWS

FINANCE COMMITTEE
ROOM 404
WILLIAM J. GOODWIN—Chairman
HENRY REGNERY
CHARLES H. MARTIN
JESSE McKEE

HOUSING COMMITTEE
ROOM 812
JULIUS E. SMIETANKA—Chairman
EDWARD A. QUINN
WILLIAM LEONARD

POLICY COMMITTEE
ROOM 411
WILLIAM A. COMSTOCK—Chairman
GEORGE F. SHORT
OTHA WEARIN
KARL CROWLEY
JOHN REGAN
JULIUS E. SMIETANKA
WILLIAM A. COMSTOCK
CHARLES H. McGLUE
JAMES A. REED
M. C. ROBERTS
MARTIN H. SWEENEY
JOHN J. O'CONNOR
WILLIAM J. GOODWIN

PUBLICITY COMMITTEE
ROOM 1619
CHARLES H. McGLUE—Chairman
JAMES R. THOMPSON
LEE MERIWETHER
RALPH MOORE
ROBERT WILLIAMS

RESOLUTIONS COMMITTEE
CONFERENCE ROOM
JAMES A. REED—Chairman
J. DuPONT THOMPSON
MARSHALL WINGFIELD
MARTIN H. SWEENEY
E. WAYLES BROWNE
OTHA D. WEARIN

RULES COMMITTEE
ROOM 1609
M. C. ROBERTS—Chairman
WILLIAM WARREN
JAMES W. MELLEN
W. P. WYNN
WALTER BOULDIN
W. R. CALLAHAN
HARVEY G. FIELDS

SPEAKERS COMMITTEE
MARTIN H. SWEENEY—Chairman
EDWARD A. QUINN
J. M. FUTRELL
MRS. WILLIAM LEONARD
ROBERT HERNDON

WAYS AND MEANS COMMITTEE
ROOM 401
JOHN J. O'CONNOR—Chairman
J. E. McDONALD
RALPH MOORE
THOMAS LINDER
CALVIN STEWART
EDWARD A. QUINN
VIRGINIA LYONS HAMILTON

504

Fields did maintain his sense of justice and fairness, and he still deplored the misuse of power. In 1943, General George Patton was one of the most confident and colorful generals to have ever served in the United States Army. He also drew the ire of the army leadership and many Americans when he visited a field hospital and found a soldier suffering from battle fatigue. Today the same disorder is part of what is classified as post-traumatic stress disorder. It is understood and is recognized as a major concern when troops return from a war zone. General Patton wasn't so understanding, and he berated and slapped the young soldier in front of many service members. Only his glowing service record kept Dwight Eisenhower from completely removing Patton from the service. Fields couldn't believe that a general officer would ever strike an enlisted man. He saw this as the same misuse of the power given by the laws of the United States government and represented what he had witnessed and fought against in Louisiana during his career. In November, he wrote Senator George protesting the incident.

November 29th, 1943.

United States Senator George,
Washington, D.C.

Dear Senator:

I am joining thousands of fathers and mothers in America, who want the truth made public as to the actions of General Patton in slapping and knocking men around and who feel that an officer of that kind is not worthy of promotion.

General Patton has had a splendid record but, evidently his nerves have gone bock on him, he must be shocked and work out and evidently is in worse condition than the men whom he slapped and knocked around and certainly the people of America should not have their boys treated that way and then have officers elevated to a higher post. We are fighting a war against cruelty, and dictatorship and if we have our boys slapped and knocked around by impatient, sick, nervous and high strung officers, then our battle is in vain.

The writer of the letter has many relatives , a son and son-in-law in the war, and had one of them in a hospital for eighteen weeks during service connection and is one hundred percent for winning the war, be he believes that we should practice democracy as well as teach it and fight for it, and it is in that spirit I am writing you in American spirit to see no officer promoted who practices things of that kind however good his record was in the past.

Yours respectfully,

Harvey G. Fields

In 1945, Fields completed his book on the assassination of Huey Long, *The Life of Huey Pierce Long.* He gave a memorial address on September 2, 1945, in his hometown of Marksville. This served as the launching of his book. Jimmy Noe had also arranged for Fields to give the memorial address over WNOE radio in New Orleans.

James A. Noe
Monroe, Louisiana

August 19, 1945

Honorable Harvey G. Fields
Farmerville, Louisiana

Dear Harvey:

In reference to your letter of August 16, first, I want to congratulate
you and Mrs. Fields on those two fine boys. When I read your letter it
took me back many years to little, ole' Doonie when he tried to ride the
cow. I could readily see then that he would have the backbone to forge
ahead. Please give both the boys my regards and tell them how proud I
am of them.

I am leaving tomorrow night for New Orleans and will take your letter up
with Jimmie Gordon. We will arrange a broadcast on August 30th, and you
will hear from Jimmie Gordan regarding this.

With best wishes, and kindest regards, I remain

Most sincerely yours,

jan;sch

Memorial Address

And Description of History
of Book Entitled

▼

"The Life of Huey Pierce Long"

BY ITS AUTHOR

Harvey G. Fields

of Farmerville, Louisiana, President of the
HUEY P. LONG MEMORIAL FOUNDATION

Delivered at Marksville, Louisiana, the Native Home and Birthplace of
Mr. Fields, and at New Orleans on September 2nd and
August 30th, 1945 respectively.

After 1945, Fields's political life would quickly decline. He continued his law practice and continued to fight for the oppressed and fight against unfair uses of power. In 1958, the Louisiana Bar Association presented Harvey Fields with an award for fifty years of continual service, practicing law as a member of the Union Parish Bar Association.

Fields received a most complimentary letter from a member of a law firm in Alexandria, Louisiana. This correspondence captured the essence and spirit of Fields's career and life.

LAW OFFICES

WARD-STEINMAN AND CRENSHAW

1128 - 5TH STREET

P. O. BOX 188

ALEXANDRIA, LOUISIANA

IRVING WARD-STEINMAN
JACK CRENSHAW

December 16th, A.D., 1 9 5 8

TEL. 3-1836

Hon Harvey G Fields, Esquire
Farmington, Louisiana

Dear and Beloved Harvey,

At last I can shout with the Latins: BRAVICCHIMO!

Your being the recipient of the accolade of honor as being a retrospective contemplation of the "Furious "'fties" warms the cockles of what is left to my heart.

Over the years your person, personality and name have been a pithy triumvirate of inspiration.

What history you made, witnessed, and analyzed.

When your memoirs are written and published, put me down for a paid copy. Title suggestion: "Thy Will Be Done, O Lord."

Am most happy that the Profession recognized a milestone and marker. What a tremendous amount of work you have accumulated as a silent kudo to your craftsmanship, integrity and brainmanship.

Your artistry as a welder of the pungent phrase and a wielder of the slugging bat against injustice is a cherished tradition to lend flame and light to those who manacle themselves to the sign of mammon.

The Dean of Attorneys!

It is the rare individual - like yourself; it is the modest accomplisher of difficult askings -like yourself; it is the humble worker against man's inhumanity to man - yourself! that I, with deep affection and reverence subscribe myself as your devoted fellow-man.

God's blessing on you, Sir Harvey!

Faithfully,

Irving Ward-Steinman

CHAPTER 8

JAMES FARLEY

From the early years of the 1920s through the 1940s, one man of strength and vision was a close friend and confidant of Fields's. This friendship was greater than the mere associations acquired through political involvement.

Behind a great politician, there is always that individual that strategically positions the person to be in a position to maximize the chances of winning an election. This is the campaign manager—that is that one person that has the managerial skills, the foresight to see what is required, and the initiative to execute a perfect campaign. One such person that epitomized the true campaign manager was James Farley.

James Farley was born in Grassy Point, New York, on May 30, 1888. His brilliant mind, coupled with his ability to improvise with innovative ideas, led to a career in politics and industry that was nothing less than miraculous. Harvey Fields met and became a friend of Farley through their association with the Democratic Party. In the nature of Harvey's personality, there was no such thing as a purely professional association, and his connection with James Farley was no exception.

Farley was a delegate to the Democratic National Convention in 1924. Harvey Fields headed the Louisiana delegation in 1928, and this service to the party, plus their associations with Franklin Delano Roosevelt, may well have been the common thread that sealed their friendship.

Like Harvey Fields, John Farley was an early entrant into the political arena. He was elected town clerk of Grassy Point in 1911 at the age of twenty-three. Seven years later, he was elected the chairman of the Rockland County Democratic Party. Farley's organizational skills secured the Democratic vote north of the Bronx Line for Al Smith, which helped Smith successfully win New York's gubernatorial race. Prior to Farley's leadership, this part of New York was not winnable by the Democratic Party. Smith was reluctant to run, but after Farley's urging, he entered the race. When Farley delivered the vote for Smith, his fate was sealed as a political mastermind. Some say Farley first met Roosevelt in 1920 during Smith's successful run for the New York governorship. This launched a political association that would continue for twenty years.

Following the Smith election, Farley was given the post of New York City port warden. Then in 1923, he was appointed to the New York Athletic Commission. A year later, Farley was at the Democratic National Convention, where he made close friends with the young Franklin Delano Roosevelt, at which time Roosevelt nominated Al Smith as the Democratic nominee for president. The 1924 nomination was unsuccessful for Smith, but neither Smith nor his political team would give up.

Farley possessed a high level of moral right. In 1926, he flexed his muscles and secured the rights for blacks to box in New York City. His leadership mandated that Jack Dempsey defend his championship by fighting an African American named Harry Wills. His directive was combined with a list of penalties that would be administered if his ruling was challenged. One dictate was that Dempsey was not allowed to fight Gene Tunney until after the fight with Wills. If his ruling was not adhered to, Tex Richard's license for his Madison Square Garden was in risk of being revoked.

The same year that Fields was leading the Louisiana delegation at the Democratic National Convention, Farley was running the 1928 gubernatorial election in New York for Franklin Roosevelt. That same year, Roosevelt successfully nominated Smith for the Democratic nominee for president at the Houston Democratic Convention. Farley worked for the Smith campaign, and this may well be the point in time that truly bonded the friendship between Farley and Fields. By 1934, Fields, as the chairman of the Louisiana Public Service Commission, was corresponding professionally with Farley.

Under the political maneuvering of Farley, Roosevelt won the race for governor. Farley was then named the secretary of the New York State Democratic Committee, and he repeated his political strategy that led to a reelection of Roosevelt in 1930. This victory caused Farley to be named the chairman of the New York State Democratic Committee.

Farley had the ability to think outside the box, which led to novel ideas that are in affect today. He understood the importance of public relations and publicity. This was a concept being used to success in Louisiana by Huey Long. Farley brought William Randolph Hearst into the Roosevelt camp. This newspaper magnate was a major accomplishment for Farley's campaign strategy. Additionally, Farley was able to capture the support of the Catholics and the unions. His earlier support for black fighter rights helped to be an asset for the Democratic Party. By cementing these diverse groups, Farley successfully provided the support required to send Roosevelt to the White House in 1932. This was the same year Richard "Dick" Leche was orchestrating a successful campaign to send Huey Long to the United States Senate.

Farley had previously predicted in public in 1930 that Roosevelt would win the 1932 election. He had set up a road trip in 1931 that covered eighteen states in nineteen days. This set the pace for future presidential elections that is considered to be a prerequisite today for any nationwide campaign. James Farley's euphoria following the election is understandable. Under his guidance, he had taken the Democratic Party and Franklin Delano Roosevelt to the highest post in the nation. A letter to Harvey Fields following the presidential election displays Farley's exuberance.

DEMOCRATIC NATIONAL CAMPAIGN COMMITTEE

HOTEL BILTMORE

NEW YORK CITY

JAMES A. FARLEY
CHAIRMAN

MURRAY HILL 2-7400

Mr. H. G. Fields   November 17, 1932
Farmerville
Louisiana

Dear Mr. Fields,

      Ours is a glorious victory, and it can be truthfully said that it was brought about by the united efforts of hundreds of thousands of Democrats in every section of this country.

      I do not think that there has ever been a time in the history of our Party when there was such a spirit of co-operation between the leaders of the Party and the rank and file. The three living former candidates for the Presidency and the Party leaders right down to our precinct and committee workers, worked zealously and unselfishly to elect our candidates. These combined efforts, supplemented by the assistance of thousands of Republican and independent voters brought about success heretofore unknown to any political party, and we all, individually, have every reason to feel proud.

      In closing, I want to thank you from my heart for the support accorded me during the entire campaign, and I want you to know that I am deeply grateful to you.

                Faithfully yours,

                C h a i r m a n

His ability to understand the electorate was brilliant as he predicted in 1936 the states that Roosevelt would carry. This was in contrast to the dire predictions of many in the Roosevelt camp.

The following letter identifies that a close bond had been built between Fields and Farley by 1939. The formality of referring to Harvey as Mr. Fields was marked out of the letter by Farley and overwritten with the less formal "Harvey."

DEMOCRATIC NATIONAL COMMITTEE
NATIONAL PRESS BUILDING
WASHINGTON

Copy sent
Blackshear

JAMES A. FARLEY
CHAIRMAN

March 16, 1939

Mr. Harvey G. Fields
Farmerville
Louisiana

Dear Mr. Fields:

      This will acknowledge your recent
letter in behalf of Mr. David Blackshear whom
you recommend for appointment to a Federal
Judgeship in the Virgin Islands.

      Your very kind letter is appreciated.
It will be associated with others of a like
character and your recommendation given every
consideration in connection with this appointment.

      With best wishes, I am

          Sincerely yours,

            Chairman

JAF:TB

Following the 1932 election, Farley was appointed to the post of United States postmaster general. It was an accepted norm at that time for an influential member of a winning presidential campaign to be presented that post. Roosevelt also appointed Farley to head the Democratic National Committee. Farley was successful at both endeavors. During this period, Farley had ties with Harvey, as well as with Jimmy Noe, former governor of Louisiana, successful businessman, and Long supporter. He also knew Earl Long, brother of Huey Long, and himself a political success.

During his tenure as postmaster general, Farley turned a governmental agency from a nonprofitable organization into an organization that was turning a profit. More amazingly was that this was accomplished during the Great Depression. He worked with Pan Am and Juan Trippe to establish effective air mail service. This he successfully instituted both domestically and internationally. Farley is credited for the introduction of the China Clipper as a method to quickly move mail across the Pacific.

Farley provided total support for Roosevelt and tirelessly worked to push through Roosevelt's first one hundred days of New Deal legislation. He drove to eliminate Prohibition and orchestrated other key legislation changes. Although he was publicly portrayed to be a leader within a liberal administration, Farley was in fact a conservative in his private beliefs. By 1940, this became apparent when cracks began appearing between him and the Roosevelt administration.

Roosevelt stated that he would not publicly seek a third term as president; however, he did indicate that if nominated, he would not decline the nomination. Farley was vocal in his disagreement over a third term for Roosevelt. Roosevelt did state that he would support Cordell Hull for president but gave Farley leave to make a run if he felt inclined to do so. This caused confusion in the Democratic ranks as there was no clear candidate that Farley could hold up to the Democratic Party.

At the 1940 convention in Chicago, Roosevelt won nomination for a third term as president of the United States. Friends and supporters of Farley nominated him for president, and he captured seventy-three votes. Roosevelt overwhelmed everyone and received 946 delegate votes. This further alienated Roosevelt, which led to Farley's resignation from both of his posts as head of the Democratic Party and as postmaster general. It is unclear if Roosevelt sought the resignation or if Farley resigned on his own.

Farley wrote Fields in 1943 and expressed his support for Hull. He referenced the 1940 election and noted that it was too bad that Hull did not win the nomination. This letter also demonstrated that Farley could be flawed in his prediction of election outcomes. His analysis of whether Roosevelt would run for another term and the predicted outcome for the Democratic Party were both in error. This is in sharp contrast to the earlier forecasts that Farley was famous for making. When considering the break with Roosevelt, the prediction in the following correspondence may express more emotion than he would have normally used.

JAMES A. FARLEY
NEW YORK

November 30, 1943

Harvey G. Fields, Esquire
Farmerville
Louisiana

Dear Harvey:

It was kind of you to take the time and trouble to write me such an interesting letter as you did on the 24th, and I want you to know that I appreciate it.   I was particularly interested in what you had to say bout Jimmie Noe's situation. The last time I saw him, which was some months ago, he indicated that under no consideration would he get out of the race.

It is also interesting to note that Congressman Morrison has them worried. He was in New York some weeks ago and he is the most confident guy I have seen in a long time.

What happens in your primary in the final outcome will have a lot to do with the way the delegates go in the National Convention. For this reason it will be very interesting to watch the situation in your State. Please continue to keep me advised.

To be very frank with you, my plans are really uncertain, but I shall keep in touch with you as to what I have in mind and as to what develops.   I am sure a great many people in Louisiana think along the same lines that you and I do. The situation around the country from a Democratic point of view is very bad. I think the Democrats will carry only about a half dozen states and then only the small ones. I think the trend is apt to get stronger rather than weaker. There is evidence of the same kind of situation that existed in 1931 when the swing was against the Republican Party. A swing is a difficult thing to stop. You retard it but you cannot stop it.

I have a sort of feeling, without anything to base it on, that the President will not run again. I think the war is about over in Europe, and when it is over the patriotic fervor for the President will disappear and he will not be even as strong as he is now. I do not know whether he realizes this or not, but this is the situation as I view it.   Mr. Hull's position before the country has improved a great deal . I do not know whether he would be interested. I am going to see him next time I am in Washington. He is a great fellow and it is too bad we did not nominate him in Chicago in 1940. He was my candidate then. I have a very high regard for him and think he is one of our great Americans.

With kindest regards and very best wishes for a pleasant holiday season,

JAF
km

Sincerely yours,

Farley spoke highly of Secretary of State Hull and would have liked to have seen him in the White House. Hull was a very capable leader and delivered the message to Japan that there were no negotiations involving China, and that the only thing that the United States would accept was a total withdrawal. On December 7, 1941, Japan delivered to Hull the infamous thirty-minute message, identifying that it would attack Pearl Harbor.

Farley was very interested in the politics of Louisiana. He understood the fervor of the Democratic Party in the state. In 1928, he visited to dedicate two new post offices in South Louisiana. Among the entourage to meet Farley was Governor Richard "Dick" Leche, who inherited the Long juggernaut in 1936 following the deaths of both Huey Long and O. K. Allen.

His dedication to the party's success, coupled with his amazing ability to remember people, their position in the party, and their potential to advance the party's cause is demonstrated in a letter to Fields in November of 1943. He specifically asked about Jimmy Noe, who took over the governorship following the death of Oscar Allen and Earl Long—Huey's brother and a former law partner of Fields's.

JAMES A. FARLEY
NEW YORK

November 10, 1943

Mr. Harvey G. Fields
Farmerville
Indiana

Dear Harvey:

Thank you very much for your letter of the 6th. I have been busy trying to catch up with the correspondence that accumulated during the election and this is the first opportunity I have had to write you.

I note what you say about supporting Morgan. I received the Shreveport paper which you forwarded to me. Please keep in touch with the situation as you see it develop and pass on anything you think will be of interest to me.

What was the reason for Earl Long stepping aside and making the race for Lieutenant Governor. I am also curious to know why Jimmie Noe stepped out of the race.

May I express the hope this letter finds your wife improved in health; and with every good wish to you both,

Sincerely yours,

JAF
km

From 1936 until 1940, Harvey Fields was not only very active in the Democratic Party, but he was also the United States attorney for the West District of Louisiana. During this period, he had become vocal about many of the New Deal policies of the Roosevelt administration. In 1941, it was questioned if he would be selected to another term as U.S. attorney despite the successes he had during his four years of serving the country. A massive mail in campaign to both Roosevelt and the attorney general saved the state from losing a highly respected federal district attorney.

When the Roosevelt/Farley split was taking place at the 1940 convention, Eleanor Roosevelt flew to Chicago to attempt to mend the rift. Her attempt proved to be fruitless as Roosevelt's betrayal of Farley could not be repaired. Although Farley remained friends with Eleanor, Fields was no supporter and publicly voiced his concern about her political position. This concern is documented in the following letter from Fields to Farley in 1946.

The letter also identifies a character trait of Fields's. He was a purist who believed in the Constitution, and that an office held by an individual should be his primary purpose in life. A trust conveyed to an elected official by the electorate required total dedication to that position. This example of dedication to position is also identified in the letter to Farley in which he criticized Supreme Court justice Jackson for not showing full devotion to this job, which Fields considered to be the final authority in the legal system. Fields was notorious for speaking out for what he thought to be right, regardless of the consequences to his personal position. Ironically, Jackson was the attorney general of the United States and the head of the Justice Department for one year when Fields was federal district attorney. Jackson had been Fields's boss.

Farmerville, Louisiana,
April 10th, 1946.

Honorable James A. Farley
Biltmore Hotel
New York City, New York.

Dear Jim:

     I see in one of the Louisiana papers this morning your name mentioned as a candidate for governor, and I hope that you will be the choice and selection of the party for that high office and it will be followed by a victory. Many of us democrats down here cannot see Robert Jackson or either Mrs.Roosevelt. I think thousands of us would rather see Dewey go back than to see Eleanor Roosevelt at the head of your state, nor to we want to see her in the United States Senate.

     Her selection as governor of New York would mean that the Democratic Party would leave entirely its traditions and principles of the past, and Jackson a dignified justice has assumed the role of an active prosecutor, while still holding his seat on the Supreme Court, and from my way of thinking is needed on the Supreme Court, and has caused justice to be thwarted by his absence, and it looks like he is seeking world-wide publicity instead of performance of duty as a justice.

     I am a loyal democrat, holding an office under a democratic administration at present, and have been nineteen times honored by my state, but I would rather see New York send a good Republican Senator than Mrs. Eleanor Roosevelt with her brand of democracy to the United States Senate.

     With kindest regards, and hoping that you are the man that is selected by the party and finally by the people, I am

                   Yours respectfully,

                   Harvey G. Fields.

When Farley left the Roosevelt administration in 1940, he quickly moved to a dynamic leadership position in industry. His early successes as postmaster general, coupled with his accomplishment of merging five small building-supply companies into the large General Builder's Corporation made Farley a highly sought-after individual. The successful company was Coca-Cola. Farley was named chairman of the board of the Coca-Cola Export Company. This is the position he held until his retirement in 1973.

Years after Farley had resigned his positions with the Roosevelt administration, Fields maintained his ties with him. In 1946, Fields had written to Farley. As was customary in a time of formal correspondence, Farley's assistant responded to a letter from Fields and noted that Farley was out of town. It was unique that the letterhead gave no indication as to Farley's position or the corporation he was connected with.

JAMES A. FARLEY
NEW YORK

Dear Mr. Fields:

            We have your letter to Mr.
Farley of April 10th, which we are holding
pending his return from Europe. We expect
him back within the next few days.

                    Very truly yours,

                    Secretary to Mr. Farley

Mr. Harvey G. Fields
Farmerville
Louisiana

April 15, 1946

When Farley returned from Europe, he responded to Fields's original correspondence. This letter did identify Farley as the chairman of the board of the Coca-Cola Export Company. Farley's shock at what he had observed in postwar Europe is apparent in the emotion contained in the following letter.

The Coca-Cola Export Corporation

515 MADISON AVENUE
NEW YORK 22, N.Y.

JAMES A. FARLEY
CHAIRMAN OF THE BOARD

April 22, 1946

Mr. Harvey G. Fields
Farmerville
Louisiana

Dear Harvey:

         Upon my return to New York your
letter of April 10th was brought to my attention. As usual, you were more than kind
in your reference to me, and I am grateful
for your confidence and friendship.

         I was abroad for eight of the past
nine weeks and had two most interesting trips
to Europe. Conditions over there are very bad,
Harvey, and I am frank to say that the devas-
tation, chaos, etc. were far beyond my imagi-
nation.

         I hope all is going well with you,
and with my very kind regards,

                     Sincerely yours,

JAF-w

When Roosevelt died in office, he was replaced by Harry Truman. Truman was a very close friend of Farley's. Farley, however, did not take the leadership roll in the Truman administration that he held with Roosevelt. This was evident from the energy required for his successful career with Coke. Following Truman's succession to the presidency, Fields wrote to Truman and had copied Farley.

The following is Farley's response to this letter. This letter may well be correspondence from Fields to Truman that pertained to the pardoning of Dick Leche following the successful prosecution in 1940 that Fields had assisted with.

The Coca-Cola Export Corporation

515 MADISON AVENUE
NEW YORK 22, N.Y.

JAMES A. FARLEY
CHAIRMAN OF THE BOARD

June 26, 1946

Dear Harvey:

Thanks for sending me a copy of your letter of June 15th to President Truman. I will be curious to see how he replies to it.

Sincerely,

Mr. Harvey G. Fields
Farmerville
Louisiana

After 1946, very little correspondence remained between Fields and Farley until 1961. Each went off in their own directions. Farley's meteoric career continued as he successfully played his part in growing Coke as a worldwide icon. It is doubtful that it was ever realized the connection of Fields's geographical home area and the area's success to James Farley's career. Delta Airlines was started in Monroe, Louisiana, as a crop-dusting business. The company's true significance as an airline was not achieved until it began carrying mail between Dallas and Atlanta in the 1930s. This opportunity was due in part to the leadership of James Farley as the postmaster general of the United States. Likewise, Monroe indirectly provided a mechanism that would help propel a future corporation that Farley would head. Coca-Cola was first bottled in Monroe under the auspices of the Biedenhorn family. The bottling of Coke made it possible to market and sell the product outside the limits of a soda stand inside the local pharmacy. Without bottling, Coke could not have been exportable. Ironically, the Biedenhorn family was also one of the founding owners of Delta.

CHAPTER 9

AND THEN HE WAS GONE

Harvey spent the 1950s practicing law and providing support to the oppressed of Farmerville and Union Parish. He had not only become an effective criminal lawyer, successfully defending several defendants in murder cases in both Louisiana and Mississippi, he had also been an efficient corporate lawyer. Among other clients, Fields was the corporate lawyer for Murphy Oil Company.

Fields was also looking at another oppressed group of Americans. The property of an African American church in Union Parish was about to be seized from the congregation. Harvey took the bold move for a white lawyer in the Deep South in the 1940s and provided legal council for the Springhill Colored Church. The church property was about to be confiscated for taxes and Harvey would not let this happen. A copy of a letter pertaining to this follows.

WARNING NOTICE

Acting as attorney and agent for the Springhill Baptist Colored Church, I hereby protest on the part of said church and for its membership, the tax sale of property under assessment No. 3468 and described as 18 acres - NE of SE Sec. Frac. 4 Twp. 23 N. R. 1 East, for the following reasons, to-wit:

That the said property belongs to the said church and religious organization, has been utilized by them over fifty years and is not assessible or subject to taxation.

That the said church is composed of colored citizens and tax payers of Union Parish, Louisiana, and is an active religious organization at present, has a number of members, a church building located thereon, together with grounds and including and adjacent to their burial ground and there has been a cemetery there for a number of years, and that a part of said land has been farmed by the Missionary Society of said church, and we hereby give notice that if said property is purchased by any outsider that the said sale will be attacked on the grounds recited above, and for other valid reasons.

Dated this June 24th, 1944.

Harvey S. Field

Attorney and agent for the
Springhill Baptist Church
Colored.

In 1958, he received his fiftieth-year award for practicing law in Union Parish. His law practice had declined to a little more than a few cases he took from people that for the most part had very little to pay. He would travel to South Louisiana and would stop numerous times to purchase a gallon of gas and visit with the station attendant. He continued his sincere enjoyment of visiting with the many individuals that made up the state. It didn't matter if the person was a governor or a laborer in the field; he enjoyed visiting with him and would talk for hours on end.

In February of 1961, his son and his ten-year-old grandson left for a business trip to the Mississippi golf course. Harvey's grandson had a strange feeling that he should run next door to tell his grandmother good-bye. He stood and looked at his grandparents' house and decided differently. Instead, he jumped in the car, and he and his father departed Farmerville. They drove partway and stopped for the night in Hattiesburg, Mississippi.

The two walked into the small restaurant at the hotel, at which time the hotel manager came to their table and said there was a phone call. The Mississippi state police wanted to talk to Thomas Sr. Young Fields stood at the large aquarium, watching the fish peacefully swimming through the water and waited for his father to return. His father soon arrived.

"Son, your grandmother has died. We need to go home." The Mississippi State had been called, and they had intercepted the two in Hattiesburg. Harvey's son drove all night long and arrived at Farmerville as the sun was rising. Immediately Harvey's grandson walked next door to see his grandfather. Numerous friends had been with him throughout the night. Harvey was sitting in his rocker in a room by himself. The grandson slowly walked into the room and threw his arms around Harvey.

In the middle of the night, Harvey's wife had walked to the kitchen sink to get a glass of water and had suddenly died from a massive heart attack. Harvey had been in town visiting some friends and found her when he arrived.

The *Monroe Morning World* had written a very poignant obituary for Harvey's wife. In Harvey's traditional manner of being the complete Southern gentleman, he wrote a letter to the editor of the paper thanking him for the nice words. This letter follows.

Harvey mourned his wife's death immensely, and he would sit up until early morning and reminisce about a time gone by. Regardless of what had happened to Fields during an extremely stressful yet exhilarating period of time, he could always count on returning home, and his beloved Evelyn would be waiting.

A month after his wife's death, he told his son he would like to go to Hot Springs, Arkansas, and stay there for a week. His son and his grandson drove with Harvey into the Ouachita Mountains, and they arrived at the popular resort town. They went to the north end of Hot Springs and pulled into the parking lot of the famous Arlington Hotel. They entered the majestic lobby of the hotel that was built in the 1920s for the pleasure of visitors from around the country.

Harvey's son checked him in, and Harvey began to query the young man that stood behind the counter. The desk clerk was well dressed in a tie and blazer and had a pleasant smile.

"Do you know if [so and so], a lawyer from Little Rock, is here?" Harvey queried. The hotel desk clerk looked puzzled and told him that he was sorry, but he didn't know him.

"Is [so and so] here? He occasionally comes up from Monroe," Harvey said. The young man was slightly uncomfortable when he told him that he didn't know the gentleman.

"Where is [so and so], a geologist with Murphy Oil?" Harvey asked with a slight annoyance. His face looked bewildered as he pointed to a chair in the hotel lobby. "He's a small man and wears glasses. He sits in that chair."

"Sir, I'm sorry. I don't recognize the man," the desk clerk disclosed.

Fields face slowly turned from frustration to sadness as he realized that the men he had spent so many years visiting with and whom he had hoped to sit and converse with about past experiences were now nothing more than ghosts living in the memory of a tired old man. Harvey's son and grandson walked him to his room and departed.

"I'll be back next Sunday and pick you up," Thomas Sr. told him. "Have a good stay, Dad."

Two days later, on an early Tuesday morning, the phone rang at Thomas Sr.'s house. "Come and get me. I'm ready to come home. There's no one left."

Thomas Sr. left Farmerville that afternoon, drove to Hot Springs, checked Harvey out of the hotel, and they returned home that evening.

Harvey's friend Tom Igoe visited him in Farmerville, and Harvey would visit Igoe's small restaurant in Simmsboro, Louisiana. Igoe used the title Colonel and had been a reporter that covered national conventions and major national news stories since the 1920s. He had retired to the small North Louisiana town and had covered the wall of his small restaurant with pictures of national leaders he had known. This was the last remnant of an amazing past that Harvey had participated in.

In 1961, Easter came in April, and April in North Louisiana is absolutely beautiful. Spring explodes into a collection of mixed color, singing birds, and warm weather. New life is leaping from all parts of nature as the dreary days of winter disappear.

On Easter morning, Thomas Sr., his wife, and his son attended church services at a local Methodist church. Harvey didn't care to go as he was not feeling well. When the family returned from the services, Thomas Sr.'s wife told him to go get Harvey for lunch. Thomas Sr.'s son bounded out in front of his father. Young Fields's hunting dog that Harvey had helped train ran behind the young boy.

Young Fields bounded through the back door to see if his grandfather felt better and if he would join the family for Easter lunch. Suddenly he froze at the door that led to Harvey's living room. A strange chill came over him, and he found he could not enter.

"You go in first," he told his father, who was trailing behind him. He did, and Harvey's grandson peeked around the corner to see the little old man that he so idolized sitting in his rocking chair, slurring his speech and trying to rise.

While Harvey's grandson stood petrified, watching his grandfather, Harvey's son ran across the street to summon Becky Post, a nurse and close family friend. Becky had met her husband in Pensacola during World War II. She was a navy nurse, and he was a marine officer. They moved to Farmerville, where her husband, Benny, eventually became president of the local bank.

Within a minute of Becky's arrival, she quietly looked at Thomas Sr. and whispered, "I think he's having a stroke."

"Dad, we need to get you to the hospital," Thomas Sr. told his father.

Harvey was able to say, "I don't need to go. I have never been to a hospital in my life," the seventy-nine-year-old disclosed.

"Mr. Harvey, Benny got sick, and we took him to the hospital," Becky told him.

Harvey's eyes flashed fire as he quickly shot back, "Ahhhh, but Ben is not the man that I am."

Harvey barely spoke after that. "Granddad, please go to the hospital," his grandson pleaded. Finally, Harvey relented. He was helped to his feet and slowly walked to a waiting ambulance. When he was walking across the back-screened porch of his house, he stopped and looked at his grandson's troubled face, managed a slight smile, and patted him on the head as if to say, "Don't worry, I will be all right."

Fields slipped into a coma that afternoon and never spoke again. Letters began coming in from around the nation, wishing him a speedy recovery.

Every afternoon, Harvey's grandson would walk the three blocks from his school to the local hospital, where he would stay until it was time to go home. Colonel Igoe would visit, as did residents of the local community.

Eventually, a feeding tube had to be inserted to provide nutrition to the old warrior. He protested as the indignant act was performed. Following several weeks of being in a coma, the prognosis was apparent, and Thomas Sr. had a difficult decision to make. Should the feeding tube be removed?

Harvey's grandson walked up to the bed. "Granddad, you need to get well. Our dog is sitting at your back door, waiting for you to come home." A sudden glimmer of recognition appeared, and that eliminated any question of removing the tube. On May 2, 1961, Harvey's grandson was allowed to stay home from school. The United States was preparing to make a bold move in the annals of history.

The grandson watched on the family's black-and-white television as a red stone rocket topped with a mercury space capsule lifted off from a pad at Cape Canaveral, Florida. While Walter Cronkite muttered "Go, baby, go," Allen Shepard became the first American to fly into space, and the U.S./Russian manned space race was on.

Young Fields returned to school and told everyone about the spaceflight. After lunch, his teacher came up to him and said, "Go, get your books. Your dad's here to pick you up."

He did as he was instructed and walked outside with his father. "Granddad died. He's gone into space with the astronaut."

Following the notice that Harvey Fields had died, letters began arriving at the residence of Thomas Sr.'s.

Laz Baughman, clerk of court for Union Parish, sent a letter of notification pertaining to the court's action to show respect for Harvey.

LAZ B. BAUGHMAN
CLERK THIRD JUDICIAL DISTRICT COURT
UNION PARISH
FARMERVILLE, LA.

JEWELL M. DAWKINS
CHIEF DEPUTY CLERK

May 16, 1961

Mr. T. T. Fields
Farmerville, Louisiana

Dear T. T.

On Monday, May 15th, 1961 the following entry was
made in Minute Book No. "P" at page 275 of the Court
Records of Union Parish, Louisiana:

Court recessed out of the Memory of the late
Harvey G. Fields, who was a member of the Union
Parish Bar Association for more than fifty years.
The Hon. J. R. Dawkins, Judge, appointed a
Special Committee, composed of Armand F. Rabun,
Chairman, Robert G. Dawkins, John C. Wagnon, James
T. Spencer and James M. Dozier Jr., all members of
the Union Parish Bar Association, to arrange for
Memorial Services to be held later in Open Court
and to draft appropriate resolutions to honor the
Memory of the late Harvey G. Fields.

If at any time I can be of service to you, please
let me know.

With personal regards, I am,

Sincerely yours

Laz B. Baughman
Clerk of Court
Union Parish, La.

P. S. - T. T., I mailed a copy of this to Mr. Fields
good friend, Colonel Tom C. Eglee of Ruston,
Louisiana.

Just prior to Harvey's death, Senator Allen Ellender wrote to express his wishes for a recovery. Ironically, Senator Ellender was one of the senators that would have been responsible for recommending Harvey for reappointment as federal district attorney.

ALLEN J. ELLENDER, LA., CHAIRMAN

OLIN D. JOHNSTON, S.C.   GEORGE D. AIKEN, VT.
SPESSARD L. HOLLAND, FLA.   MILTON R. YOUNG, N. DAK.
JAMES O. EASTLAND, MISS.   BOURKE B. HICKENLOOPER, IOWA
HERMAN E. TALMADGE, GA.   KARL E. MUNDT, S. DAK.
WILLIAM PROXMIRE, WIS.   JOHN SHERMAN COOPER, KY.
B. EVERETT JORDAN, N.C.   J. CALEB BOGGS, DEL.
STEPHEN M. YOUNG, OHIO
PHILIP A. HART, MICH.
EUGENE J. MCCARTHY, MINN.
MAURINE B. NEUBERGER, OREG.

COTYS M. MOUSER, CHIEF CLERK

United States Senate

COMMITTEE ON
AGRICULTURE AND FORESTRY

April 17, 1961

<u>AIR MAIL</u>

Dear Harvey:

I have just learned that you are in the hospital, after being stricken on Easter Sunday. I was in Shreveport on Monday and Tuesday after Easter, but I did not learn of your illness when I was there.

This is just a note to express my sympathy, and to let you know that I am thinking about you. I do hope you will soon be well on the road to recovery, and that I will have the pleasure of seeing you when I get to Union Parish on my annual tour of the State this fall.

With kindest personal regards and best wishes, I am

Sincerely,

ALLEN J. ELLENDER
U. S. Senator

Mr. Harvey G. Fields
Norris-Booth Clinic
Farmerville, Louisiana

Several of the Louisiana Supreme Court justices sent letters to Thomas.

Supreme Court
STATE OF LOUISIANA
New Orleans

May 8, 1961.

CHIEF JUSTICE
JOHN B. FOURNET
ASSOCIATE JUSTICES
JOE B. HAMITER
FRANK W. HAWTHORNE
E. HOWARD McCALEB
WALTER B. HAMLIN
JOE W. SANDERS
FRANK W. SUMMERS

Hon. T. T. Fields,
Farmerville, La.

Dear T. T.:

Stella and I desire to extend our deepest sympathy to you
and your family upon your father's passing. He was indeed
a good friend of mine for many years, and I profited greatly
throughout the years by reason of his good advice and his
fine philosophy.

I was informed just the other day of your mother's passing,
and we desire to extend our deepest sympathy upon her passing,
also.

With kindest regards to you and yours, in which Stella joins
me, I remain,

Sincerely yours,

Walter

Fields had been a very loyal supporter of Huey Long and his programs aimed at bettering the lives of the typical American. Long's son, Russell, was elected to the Senate of the United States and was a very effective member of the Senate throughout his career.

RUSSELL B. LONG
LOUISIANA

United States Senate
WASHINGTON, D. C.

May 16, 1961

Honorable T. T. Fields
Farmerville
Louisiana

Dear T. T.:

Word reached me recently of your father's death,
and I want to express to you my deepest sympathy and to
let you know that I share your loss.

As you know, your father was one of the best friends
that my family ever had and many of us will miss him.

Certainly you should be consoled by the knowledge
of the tremendous good he did for our state and the great
respect in which he was held by so many.

With all good wishes, I am

Sincerely yours,

Russell

Fields was associated with members of the United States Supreme Court. One of
these was Tom Clarke, former United States attorney general, Supreme Court justice,
and father of Ramsey Clarke, who was also a United States attorney general.

Supreme Court of the United States
Washington 25, D. C.

CHAMBERS OF
JUSTICE TOM C. CLARK   May 8, 1961

Mr. T. T. Fields
Farmerville
Louisiana

Dear Mr. Fields:

I have just learned that my very dear friend

Harvey Fields has passed away and I hasten to extend

my sympathy. Having lost my father I know full well

what it means at this time. But, he has left you a

great heritage and I am sure you must in reflecting

on this, be greatly comforted.

If I can assist with anything I do hope you

will let me know.

Sincerely,

Tom C. Clark ✓

At the time of Fields's death, Orval Faubus was governor of Arkansas. Faubus's reference to Fields as being a fine gentleman would have pleased Harvey. That was a hallmark Fields placed above all other attributes.

STATE OF ARKANSAS
OFFICE OF THE GOVERNOR
LITTLE ROCK

ORVAL E. FAUBUS
GOVERNOR

May 16, 1961

Mr. T. T. Fields
Farmerville, Louisiana

Dear Mr. Fields:

I was very grieved to learn of the death of your father,
Harvey G. Fields. There is very little anyone can say
or do at such a time, but I did want you to know that you
and your family have my deepest sympathy.

Your state and the nation will sorely miss your father.
He was not only a fine public servant, but also an outstanding gentleman in the truest sense of the word.
He left you a legacy of service of which you may well be
proud, and has gone on to merited rewards.

If at any time I may be of assistance to you, you have
but to call on me.

Most sincerely,

Orval E. Faubus
Governor

OEF:dh

Overton Brooks was associated with Harvey since Harvey was in the state senate
in 1912. His reference to Harvey's fiery spirit epitomizes Fields's entire life. Overton
Brookes should not be confused with Senator Overton that Fields had helped to get
elected.

HOUSE OF REPRESENTATIVES
WASHINGTON, D. C.

OVERTON BROOKS
4TH DISTRICT, LOUISIANA   May 16, 1961

Honorable T. T. Fields
State Representative
Farmerville, Louisiana

Dear Friend:

I wish to express the sadness which was mine
when I learned of the loss of your father,
Harvey Fields. Just before I left Shreveport
sometime back I had the opportunity of visiting with him. He still had the same fighting
spirit that characterized him when I first met
him in the State Legislature, somewhere around
the year 1912, when I was a page there. During
his entire life he was always a fighter for
that which he felt was right.

In this dark hour of your sorrow I wish to extend to you, Harvey, Jr., Mrs. Copeland and
in fact all the members of the family my deep
and abiding sympathy in your heavy loss.

                              Very sincerely your friend,

                              Overton Brooks, M. C.

OB:wrh

Ernest Clements was the chairman of the Louisiana Public Service Commission at the time of Harvey's death. This was the same position that Harvey held when he had so successfully crafted a commission that was free of corruption and dedicated to providing public services to the residents of Louisiana.

ALL FILES, RECORDS AND DATA IN GENERAL OFFICES, BATON ROUGE, LA.

STATE OF LOUISIANA

ERNEST S. CLEMENTS, CHAIRMAN
OBERLIN

NAT B. KNIGHT, JR., COMMISSIONER
1011 FOURTH STREET
GRETNA

JOHN J. McKEITHEN, COMMISSIONER
MONROE

CLAYTON W. COLEMAN, SECRETARY

SAMUEL I. NICHOLS, DIRECTOR, UTILITIES DIVISION

LOUISIANA PUBLIC SERVICE COMMISSION

IN REPLY PLEASE REFER
TO OUR FILE NO.

Oberlin, Louisiana
May 14, 1961.

Hon. T. T. Fields,
State Representative,
State Capitol,
Baton Rouge, Louisiana.

Dear Friend:

      I was so sorry to learn, through
the medium of the press, of the untimely passing
of your dear father, and hasten to extend to you
and your family my sincere sympathy.

      It was my good fortune to have known
your father for many years, and I always enjoyed
talking with him.

      With assurances again of my deepest
sympathy, I am

            Sincerely,

            Ernest S. Clements.

In 1961, John McKeithen was a member of the Louisiana Public Service Commission. In 1968, he would become the governor of Louisiana. At that time, Thomas Fields was elected to his fourth term as state representative and served under McKeithen.

ALL FILES, RECORDS AND DATA IN GENERAL OFFICES, BATON ROUGE, LA.

STATE OF LOUISIANA

ERNEST S. CLEMENTS, CHAIRMAN
OBERLIN

NAT B. KNIGHT, JR., COMMISSIONER
1011 FOURTH STREET
GRETNA

JOHN J. McKEITHEN, COMMISSIONER
MONROE

CLAYTON W. COLEMAN, SECRETARY

SAMUEL I. NICHOLS, DIRECTOR, UTILITIES DIVISION

LOUISIANA PUBLIC SERVICE COMMISSION

IN REPLY PLEASE REFER
TO OUR FILE NO.

Monroe, Louisiana
May 8, 1961

Honorable T. T. Fields
State Representative
Union Parish
Farmerville, Louisiana

Dear T. T.:

    Please accept my sincere sympathy and condolences in
the passing of your father. He had the respect of all
who knew him. He had rightfully earned it and was truly
a great man.

    I am sorry I missed you Thursday when I was in Farmerville
and I look forward to seeing you soon.

    With kindest personal regards, I am

                 Sincerely your friend,

                 John J. McKeithen
                 Commissioner

JJMcK:jb

Gene Talmadge was a four time governor of Georgia that lived the hard fisted autocratic style of the Huey Long mold. He and Fields had been friends for years and both had a hard core dislike of the Roosevelt New Deal Policy. Talmadge once described the New Deal policy as "a combination of wet nursing, frenzied finance, downright Communism and plain damn foolishness". *Time* Magazine commented that Talmadge was only eclipsed by Mississippi's Theodore Bilbo and Louisiana's Huey Long for so successfully appealing to ignorance and bigotry. It was also noted that following his loss of the governor's post in 1942 that his defeat "ended the reign of the most high-handed, low browed local dictator that U.S. politics has known since the days of the late Huey Long". Gene was re-elected in 1946 but died of cirrhosis of the liver before he could take office.

At one of the Democratic conventions, Fields had taken on the Honorable Carter Glass in defense of the seating of Gene Tallmadge. Fields won, and Tallmadge was seated. This was Fields's second defeat of Glass on a convention floor and ended any future confrontation. Tallmadge's son, Herman, followed in his father's footsteps. He wrote to Harvey when Harvey was stricken and to Thomas Sr. following Harvey's death.

HERMAN E. TALMADGE
GEORGIA

COMMITTEES:
AGRICULTURE AND FORESTRY
FINANCE

United States Senate
WASHINGTON, D. C.

Dear Mr. Fields:

It was with regret that I learned from
our mutual friend, Honorable Tom Igoe
of Ruston, of your illness. I trust
that your condition is not serious and
that you will enjoy a speedy and permanent
recovery.

Also, permit me to take this opportunity
to express to you and your family the
appreciation of all of the Talmadges for
your friendship over the years. It is
certainly our hope that we shall always
be able to merit it.

Please do not hesitate to let me know
whenever I may be of assistance, and
with kindest regards, I am

Sincerely,

Herman E. Talmadge

Honorable Harvey G. Fields
c/o Honorable T. T. Fields
Farmerville, Louisiana

21 April 1961

HERMAN E. TALMADGE
GEORGIA

COMMITTEES:
AGRICULTURE AND FORESTRY
FINANCE

United States Senate
WASHINGTON, D.C.

Dear Friends:

Mr. Tom C. Igoe of Ruston, Louisiana,
has just advised me of the passing
of your loved one.

Please accept and extend to each member
of the family my deepest sympathy upon
the great loss you have suffered.

With kindest regards, I am

Sincerely,

Herman E. Talmadge

The Family of
  Honorable Harvey G. Fields
c/o Honorable T. T. Fields
Farmerville, Louisiana

6 May 1961

Another person whose friendship went back to the time that Harvey was in the
Louisiana state senate was Dr. David E. Brown, who served with Harvey in the 1912
to 1916 Louisiana senate.

DAVID E. BROWN, M. D.
DIRECTOR

Louisiana State Department of Health
City-Parish Health Unit
PARISH OF EAST BATON ROUGE
CITY OF BATON ROUGE
1813 FLORIDA STREET
BATON ROUGE 1, LA.

May 15, 1961

Mr. T. T. Fields
House of Representatives
Baton Rouge, Louisiana

Dear Mr. Fields:

I wish to extend to you and family my sincere sympathy in this hour of sorrow in the death of your father.

He and I were close friends for many years. We were in the State Senate together from 1916 to 1920 and were close friends ever since, to the day of his death. My half-brother, Edgar Ewing of Ruston, was also a close friend of your father.

With best wishes, I am

Sincerely,

David F. Brown, M. D.

P.O. Box 830

James Farley—political manager of monumental proportions, former head of the National Democratic Central Committee, former postmaster general of the United States, chairman of the board of Coca-Cola Export Company, and friend of Harvey Fields—wrote to Thomas.

JAMES A. FARLEY
NEW YORK

May 10, 1961.

Dear Mr. Fields:

    It grieved me very much to learn from
our mutual friend, Mr. Thomas C. Igoe of Ruston,
of your father's passing, and I offer you my heartfelt sympathy in your loss and sorrow.

    While I knew that his illness was serious
I did not look for his death so soon, and I feel
deeply about it for as you know we were truly great
friends for over thirty years. I thoroughly enjoyed
the correspondence I had with him down through the
years, although it has been some time since our paths
crossed. Your father was a fine citizen, and I can
appreciate what his passing means to all who came within the range of his influence.

                 Sincerely yours,

Honorable T. T. Fields,
Farmerville,
Louisiana.

Suite 1800
515 Madison Ave
New York 22, N.Y.

And then there was one. Huey Long died in 1935. In 1960, Earl Long died,
following his election to the United States Senate. This left only one survivor of
the law firm that took on big business and provided legal services for the exploited
individuals of the state. This person was Judge Robert O'Neal, member of the First
District Court of Louisiana.

JUDGES

ROBERT J. O'NEAL
HENRY F. TURNER
WILLIAM F. WOODS, JR.
JOHN A. DIXON, JR.

FIRST DISTRICT COURT of LOUISIANA

PARISH OF CADDO

SHREVEPORT, LOUISIANA

May 8, 1961.

Mr. T. T. Fields,

Farmerville, La.

Dear Sir and Friend:

      I note with regret the passing of
your father and extend to you and family my sincere
sympathy. He lived a long and usefull life and
you children have much to be proud of. I enjoyed
our association together and in writing him when your
mother passed away, I said that I would come to see him
the next time I went down to the old home place at Choudrant.
We never know what to expect. I have had the misfortune
to lose three in my family in the past six weeks.

      Trusting that I may have the pleasure
of seeing you in the future, and with personal regards, I am,

          Yours truly,

Harvey had spent his life as a fighter for justice and a defender of the rights of individuals. He relished the thought of successfully bringing relief to people that had been oppressed in one manner or the other. At his death, the family received words of sorrow and praise from individuals that were in senior positions of the government, the legal profession, and the industry. However, for a person that received so much enjoyment from the knowledge that he had helped the exploited, there was nothing so poignant than what took place on the afternoon of his death.

The United States has dramatically changed since 1961. The civil rights of everyone has made phenomenal strides since that year. In 1961, there was a white drinking fountain and a black drinking fountain at the courthouse in Farmerville, as there were also segregated public restrooms. There was a black high school in the black southern section of town, and no white child would go there. There was also a white school in the middle of town, and it was unheard of for a black child to enter those school grounds. Blacks attended the black churches, and whites would attend white churches. There was a white funeral home and a black funeral home, and neither would be visited by members of the other race. Rosa Parks had as yet not made her valiant stand on a bus in Birmingham.

Thomas Sr. knew Harvey's end was in sight long before he died, and he had made arrangements for the services well in advance. He wanted visitation the night of the death and the burial the next day. It was announced around town that visitation would be the evening that Harvey had died.

Harvey passed away at 1:00 PM, and visitation would take place at 6:00 PM. Late in the afternoon of Harvey's death, the phone rang at the Fields residence. It was a leader of the black community, and he had a request for Fields. Members of the Farmerville black community would like to pay their final respects to "Lawyer Fields." This was unprecedented, and Thomas said he would get back to him with a response. Fields called the funeral home and talked to the owner, who was a lifelong friend of Harvey's and his family. That night, visitation occurred as scheduled, and at 9:00 PM, the front doors of the funeral home were closed and locked. Then someone quietly walked to the back door of the funeral home and unlocked it. Members of the black community then entered to pay their final respects to Harvey Fields. A tribute that Fields would have deeply appreciated.

Fields left a legacy of continued community service and support for the oppressed. Fields's youngest son, Harvey Jr., attended Tulane following his discharge from the U.S. Navy. He was elected president of the student body, played football, and later obtained his law degree. Junior eventually lived in Los Angeles, where he was a successful public defendant. Thomas Sr. returned to Farmerville following his discharge from the U.S. Army. He became a successful businessman in the timber industry. He also carved out a very successful political career as a state representative. Some of his major accomplishments were the introduction of the legislation for the construction of Lake D'Aarbonne, obtaining one of the first state vocational technical schools in North Central Louisiana, supporting an aggressive paving program for state roads in Union Parish, and cosponsoring legislation that provided university status for Northeast Louisiana State College, Louisiana Polytechnical Institute, and Grambling College.

Following the funeral, Harvey Jr. left for Los Angeles. Harvey Jr. wrote Thomas upon his return and noted that they had a great legacy given to them by Harvey, but he did wish that Harvey could have been around a little more while they were growing up. He was philosophical in noting that considering the good that was accomplished, this would have to be acceptable.

CHAPTER 10

A FITTING EPITAPH

On May 8, 1961, the *Ruston Daily Leader* carried on its front page the story of the first American to travel into space. Allen Shepard, astronaut and American hero, would have to share that page with Harvey Fields. Tom Igoe, political writer since the 1920s, wrote the final epitaph for Harvey.

> *This assignment is approached, not so much in the traditional role of a reporter but rather through the graciousness of the Publisher and Editor, it takes the form of a "Hail and Farewell" to an old and cherished friend and to North Louisiana's First Citizen.*
>
> *The month of May marks the occasion of two memorable events—a birthday into the world of a man at Marksville, Louisiana, on the thirty-first, 1882, and another 79 years later into Life Eternal, of Harvey G. Fields at one past noon, Friday, May 5th, at Farmerville.*
>
> *The memory of his life and unselfish service can never die from out of the heart of the people of Farmerville, of Louisiana and of the nation's great who knew and loved him. It "affords a ballast 'gainst all the storms that blow. And although it lends unspeakable sadness, it imparts a quiet peace.*
>
> MARRIED EVELYN SANDERS. *By this very nature Harvey Fields was too decidedly masculine, that is to say, one sided, to exist long without the love of a woman; his wife Evelyn Sanders Fields, gentle, generous, motherly, plastic, needed him no less than he needed her, and when her spirit passed away, preceding him by three months to the day, he really never recovered from the shock which unnerved him.*

> ### NOTED LAWYER
>
> *Among the Nation's really big men in the fields of politics and of law, the name of Harvey G. Fields, the man and Farmerville, the town in Union Parish, Louisiana, are almost one and inseparable in their thought and speech.*
>
> *When Harvey Fields' tired and deep furrowed face looked for the last time, up at the morning sun, God, understandingly said to Gabriel, "Here comes a man."*

The easiest way to establish fact is to take a peek into his personal files and find out who were his friends and admirers. The reporter found letters from Theodore Roosevelt, William Howard Taft, Woodrow Wilson, William Gibbs McAdoo, Elibu Root, Arthur Brisbane, Edward Everett Hale, John H. Patterson, Tom L. Johnson, Ogden Armour, Elbert Gary, Clarence Darrow, James A. Farley, Franklin D. Roosevelt, Bennett Champ Clarke, Jim Reed, Ed Crump, Gene Talmadge, Harry F. Byrd, Richard B. Russell, Tom Heflin, Wm. Borsch, Homer Cummings, and Tom Clarke.

In his private files are epistles from presidents, cabinet officers, literary lights, United States senators, congressmen, railroad presidents, businessmen, educators, and actors. He knew them all, and they knew him.

LETTERS POUR IN

When following his confinement to the hospital on Easter Sunday, word went abroad that Mr. Fields had been probably fatally stricken. Letters, telegrams, and followers were directed to Harvey, to his son T. T. Fields, and the Fields family from over all the nation; from old and faithful friends they poured in until the hour of interment at three o'clock Saturday afternoon.

Here are a few offered excerpts from a few such letters:

> *I have just received a letter from my good friend Tom Igoe, in which he told me of the illness of your father. I have known your father for over 30 years. He is a dear friend and one for whom I have great admiration and affection and I have enjoyed the correspondence I have had with him down through the years.*
>
> *Sincerely Yours,*
> *James Farley*

> *I am sorry to learn of your father's illness. If now or ever there be anything that I or the Talmadge family or the State of Georgia can do for your father or his family please do call on me.*
>
> *Herman Talmadge*
> *U.S. Senator, Georgia*

> *I was glad to have your letter. Of course I remember Harvey Fields very well. He was an able citizen around a convention . . . There is one encounter I remember that Fields had with Carter Glass. That was at the Democratic National Convention at Houston in 1928. Col. Robert Ewing of New Orleans, who was an original ally of Huey Long, and Fields carried the battle to seat the Long Delegation over a delegation headed by Col James Thompson of New Orleans. The Long delegation, against which Carter Glass led the fight was seated . . . I have missed a lot of things around*

conventions as they are a three-ring circus and it is impossible to be everywhere. I
hope Harvey Fields is soon restored to good health.

Sincerely,

Bascom N. Timmons

National Press, Washington, D.C.

SOME HISTORIC CASES

During his long and active life, Harvey Fields served as United States attorney for the Northern District of Louisiana. He was appointed to the post by Franklin D. Roosevelt. With one O. John Rogge, he prosecuted and convicted former governor Leche and his colleagues Abe Shushan and Seymour Weiss, et al. In that case particularly, the blackberry bush Blackstones sat upon him, as the coroners would say, with intent to low-rate and disparage; but as always, when before the court, he made the older, easygoing members of the bar feel to see whether their laurel wreaths were in place.

Methods of crime change; the use of the law to catch criminals should change accordingly. The mail fraud statutes were classic, he recalled from past, not-too-close acquaintance with them. But he looked into the subject, and he stretched their elasticity to an extent that made contemporary criminal precedence. He clamped the fraud upon the offenders, and on top of that, he clamped a charge of using the mails in connection with it. They had cheated the state, to be sure; but they themselves hooked the federal government into the act. He contended that the federal aspects of the cases permitted the Department of Justice to exercise an "educational function" to demonstrate to Louisiana how its public affairs were being managed. He went to work, then to teach everything he knew on the subject. And what he taught might well serve as a refresher course for the contemporary corps of politicos. The offenders were duly convicted and served their time with reduction for good behavior.

It is interesting commentary that in the case of Governor Leche, when he became eligible for parole, it was Harvey Fields that made the trip to Washington at his own expense to plead to the attorney general on behalf of the man he convicted only a few years earlier. The Fields plea won freedom for the ex-governor. On Saturday, an hour before the final rights were to be held for Harvey Fields, the telephone rang in the T. T. Fields residence. The operator said this is long distance calling. Mr. T. T. Fields, and it was ex-governor Leche on the line, expressing regrets over the passing of an old friend who had never wavered in line of duty regardless of personal sentiment in another direction, assuring the son that he bore only the utmost of respect and goodwill toward his father. And thus, Dick Leche won the admiration of this reporter and the family and friends present in the Fields home.

Then a reporter assigned to the Democratic National Convention in New York during the heyday of the Harvey G. Fields leadership of the Louisiana delegation (1928-1940), I recall a bitter floor fight by and between Mr. Fields and the Honorable Carter Glass of Virginia, when O'Connor, the Tammany Hall powerhouse politician tried to have "Gene Talmadge" read out of the convention, because if memory serves, he, Talmadge, refused preconvention endorsement of the party candidate and platform. It looked bad for the gallus-snapping delegate from Georgia.

Glass was a great orator and a master at sarcasm. He made one fatal mistake—he underestimated Fields. When the oratorical fireworks was over, and the floor vote of the convention was tabulated, Fields won for Talmadge. I can see "Old Gene" now as he walked up to Fields on the platform, threw his arms around him, and wept salt tears of gratitude. As I recall, the Talmadge vote margin was by a goodly eighteen votes.

And so, one who knew and followed him through the years, as I did, from the 1928 convention in Houston, through successive ones in Chicago, Philadelphia, and New York could go on and on almost endlessly. Then, too, there were those earlier days we spent together with Clarence Darrow, Dudley Field Malone, Arthur Garfield Hayes, and William Jennings Bryan at Cleveland, Tennessee, during the alleged Scopes Monkey Trial where there was much hilarity, feats of wit, and flow of soul. Fields asked of Darrow and said, "What are you trying to do with old man Bryan, anyway?" (Bryan was fighting for the teachings of the church against the theory of evolution.) Darrow laughed and said, "Now, Fields, you stay out of this. We can best Bryan, but I am afraid of you. We won't hurt the old commoner too much, but we do want to make him admit, for the sake of the record, that he actually believes that Jesus Christ had but one parent."

"And when you accomplish that, what then?" queried Fields. "Then the trial will be over," said Darrow. "When then do Scopes and the evolution theory come in?" pressed Fields. "It doesn't," parried Darrow. "That being the case, you, three distinguished gentlemen have perpetuated an unholy farce upon the people of Tennessee and the nation and with me. The trial is, and was, over even before it got under way." After this, on July 26, 1925, the Great Bryan died in his sleep following a heavy lunch, and even the three agnostics shed salt tears with us over the passing of the nation's silver-tongued orator.

And I still call him Granddad.

Six months after Harvey Fields died, his friend Tom C. Igoe died peacefully in his sleep in Simmsboro, Louisiana. In accordance with his wishes, he was cremated, and his ashes were spread over his flower gardens at his beloved restaurant.

The Harvey G. Fields papers were offered to and gratefully accepted by the Louisiana State University Library, where they have now been archived for the use and benefit of future generations.

EPILOGUE

- Following the research for the book the author visited with his cousin who was raised by Harvey for the cousin's last three high school years. The cousin was amazed with what the author told him. He stated that he would spend time with Harvey sitting in front of the fireplace in Harvey's living room. Harvey would talk about the flag and patriotism and the United States but not once did he ever disclose any of his past accomplishments nor any of his past associations.

BIBLIOGRAPHY

- Williams, T. Harry. *Huey Long*. Knopf, 1969. (Winner of the 1970 Pulitzer Prize and the National Book Award)
- Fields, Harvey Goodwin. *The Life of Huey Pierce Long*. Fields Publishing, 1946.
- Fields, Harvey G. The 1944-45 edition of *Who's Who in America—Who's Who in American Politics* and *Who's Who in the South*.

EXTERNAL LINKS

- Wikipedia—Earl Long
- Earl Long Notes
- Thepineywoods.com—Earl Longshore
- Inside North side—Uncle Earl Crazy bout the North
- Wikipedia—Huey Long
- Social Security Online—Huey Long
- Social Security Online Huey Long's Senate Speeches
- Hueylong.com—Louisiana After Long
- Wikipedia—1924 Democratic National Convention
- Wikipedia—William Jennings Bryan
- Projects.vassar.edu—William Jennings Bryan
- Encyclopedia.com—William Jennings Bryan
- Wikipedia—Clarence Darrow
- Wikipedia Butler Act
- Wikipedia—Share Our Wealth
- Wikipedia—Riley J. Wilson
- Digital History—The Election of 1928
- Wikipedia—Leon C. Weiss
- Wikipedia—Tom C. Clark
- Wikipedia—Cordell Hull
- Answers.Com—Bankhead Cotton Act
- Wikipedia—National Recovery Administration
- Rooseveltmyth.com Chapter Six—The Dance of the Crackpots
- Encyclopedia of Arkansas—Hattie Wyatt Caraway
- Encyclopedia of Arkansas—Charles Hillman Brough
- American Heritage.com—The Long, Long Trail

- Wikipedia—Hugh Samuel Johnson
- Wikipedia—Carter Glass
- Wikipedia—1932 Democratic National Convention
- Wikipedia—United States Presidential Election, 1932
- Presidency.ucsb.edu—Democratic Party Platform of 1928
- Wikipedia—Theodore G. Bilbo
- Historymatters.gmu.edu—Should a Catholic Be President: A Contemporary View of the 1928 Election
- Wikipedia—1928 Democratic National Convention
- Wikipedia—New Deal
- Wikipedia—Oscar K. Long
- Wikipedia—Blanche Long
- Wikipedia—1936 Democratic National Convention
- Wikipedia—James A. Noe
- Time.com June 22, 1936, Southwest Swing
- Time.com—May 10, 1937, For Tarpon
- Time.com—April 18, 1938, Coliseum Fracas
- Time.com—July 3, 1939, Huey's Boy Friends
- Time.com—July 17, 1939, One Was a Son-of-a-Gun
- Time.com—July 31, 1939, Rats in the Pantry
- Time.com—August 14, 1939, Jughead v. the U.S.
- Time.com—Sept 25, 1939, One Down
- Time.com—Feb. 26, 1940, Lonesome Man
- Time.com—Apr. 8, 1940, Progress
- Time.com—Nov 4, 1946
- National Governor's Association—Richard Webster Leche
- Wikipedia—Seymour Weiss
- Expedia—Louisiana 1938
- Expedia—Louisiana 1939
- Time.com—January 30, 1928, Louisiana Governor
- Time.com—December 18, 1933, Revolting Parishes
- Time.com—April 30, 1934, Sixth's third
- Time.com—Sept 21, 1942, Exit Gene Talmadge
- Time.com—Dec 30, 1946, Death of the Wild Man
- Wikepedia—Bolivar Kemp
- Wikepedia—Pat Parrison
- Conservapedia—Pat Harrison
- Bioguide..congress—Harrison, Byron Patton
- Spartacus.schoolnet.co.uk—Eugene Talmadge
- Ourgeorgiahistory.com—Eugene Talmadge\
- msbar.org—W. Calvin Wells
- politicalgraveyard—Harvey G. Fields

- Wikipedia—Scopes Monkey Trial
- Americanrhetoric.com/speeches/fdrfirstinaugural
- Wikepedia—William Gibbs McAdoo